SLOBODSKAYA

A Biography of Oda Slobodskaya

SLOBODSKAYA

A Biography of Oda Slobodskaya

by

MAURICE LEONARD

LONDON
VICTOR GOLLANCZ LTD
1979

ISBN 0 575 02622

PRINTED IN GREAT BRITAIN
BY EBENEZER BAYLIS AND SON LTD
THE TRINITY PRESS, WORCESTER, AND LONDON

"Such a glorious voice as this would make a poem of an income tax form."

SIR COMPTON MACKENZIE

"Together with many others, I am overjoyed that this book will again bring her near to us, so that we may relive our memories. We were all enriched by her presence and will not forget her."

DAME EVA TURNER

ACKNOWLEDGEMENTS

In addition to everyone mentioned in this book, thanks are due to Christine Bolton, Betty Drake, Cyril Franklin; and particularly to the Baroness Olink for her continued encouragement throughout.

CONTENTS

A section of photographs follows page 96.

PART ONE

The War Horse :
Personal Recollections

PERSONAL RECOLLECTIONS

THE OLD LADY with a withered flower-garden for a hat peered at me across the counter. Working in the HMV Record Shop in Oxford Street was a hard slog, particularly at the end of the day, so I looked away, hoping she'd move on. Her pale blue coat was faded and looked grubby and she had a surly look on her face.

But she was persistent and when, eventually, I looked round, her beady eye was still on me, determined to get my attention. I tried to walk away but she grabbed my sleeve with a none too gentle finger and thumb.

"What?" I demanded.

"What Slobodskaya records have you got?" Her voice was deep, almost like a man's, with a pronounced accent. I knew the name she mentioned as we stocked *The Art of Oda Slobodskaya* in our *Great Singers of the Past* section. It was a particularly memorable sleeve with a sepia photograph of Madame Slobodskaya looking exactly as though it had been plucked from some Edwardian mantelpiece. Her figure was tall and imposing and she wore a shiny gown with a train, her hair was swept back and hands clasped regally to her bosom. A jardinière of potted plants was in the background.

I fished out the record sleeve and handed it to her but her disagreeable expression did not alter.

"Have you any others?" she asked and, again, her deep voice surprised me. I told her there was nothing else.

Turning down the corners of her mouth she jabbed her breast with a thumb and announced, "I Slobodskaya." She said it as though telling me she had cancer.

I looked at the record sleeve and back at her. Then a blurred resemblance seemed to form between the two faces, it was mainly the black, slanting eyes and the Mongolian cheekbones. Presumably her accent was Russian.

"No one buys my records now," she intoned funereally. I didn't know how to answer because it was true. Handing me back the record sleeve she walked out of the shop, the flowers flopping on her hat.

I had never bothered to play the Slobodskaya record but, that evening, out of curiosity, I did so and was impressed by her powerful, heavy soprano.

I did not expect to see her again but I never forgot her. She began to fascinate me. I took the record home and played it frequently until I came to know the voice well.

A friend told me that she had been so famous at one time that she had never been off the radio, and the *Radio Times* used to publish pictures of her wearing unbelievably long ear-rings. But that was years ago, she'd not been heard of recently.

It was, therefore, with some surprise when I saw her name advertised for a concert at the Royal Festival Hall. She was to perform on Sunday 10 May 1964 at 7.30 pm with John Pritchard conducting the London Philharmonic Orchestra. She was not singing but narrating *Peter and the Wolf*. I had to go.

She was wearing a similar dress to the shiny one on the record cover. Ornaments were sprinkled over her arms and bodice and she wore long ear-rings. With the aid of a lorgnette she read from a score. The reviewer for *The Sunday Times* summed up her performance in a sentence, "Colourful narrator Oda Slobodskaya immediately filled the hall with her presence".

One summer's evening, some weeks later, I saw her in Baker Street, looking in the window of an antique shop. The blue coat had been exchanged for a brown one with flared mediaeval sleeves; the middle-ages effect was enhanced by a piece of floating tulle attached to a conical hat. I introduced myself and she slowly and formally curtsied. I told her I enjoyed her Festival Hall appearance and remarked that her dress then was similar to the one on the record sleeve. She told me it was the same. I invited her for a cup of coffee at a nearby café, which she refused, but added, "I would love a milk stout." So we went to the Volunteer pub opposite and spoke of music. Some of the conversation was difficult to follow due to the screeches of the publican's parrot, which sat in a cage in the saloon, thriving on the alcohol and tobacco fumes.

After our drinks we left the pub and crossed the road to Regent's Park and I looked for a deckchair that wasn't covered in bird droppings for her to sit on. After finding one I pulled up another for myself and sat next to her. We sat for a long time and she was charming and interesting. She held her collar up to her throat the whole time, despite the strong sunshine. Among other things she told me that a singer must firstly know her music, secondly always be true to the composer's intentions, and thirdly, most importantly, she must love it.

I walked her back to Ivor Court, a block of flats near Baker Street. Before we parted she handed me her card and as soon as she had gone I scrutinized it:

ODA SLOBODSKAYA F.G.S.M.

Marynsky Opera, Petrograd
La Scala, Milan
Royal Opera, Covent Garden, London
Colon Theatre, Buenos Aires

Professor of Singing Guildhall School and Royal College of Music. Specialist in Russian Repertoire. Lecture Recitals on Russian Songs.

RECORDINGS INCLUDE

DECCA LXT 5663 The Art of Oda Slobodskaya
CEP 5500 Shostakovitch – Six Spanish Songs
CEP 5501 Kabalevsky – Seven Nursery Songs
SAGA XID 5050 Russian Songs – recital Vol 1
XID 5069 Russian Songs – recital Vol 2
DELTA 12004 Chopin – Nineteen Polish Songs
ATL 4102 Prokofiev – Peter and the Wolf
Narration by Oda Slobodskaya

60, Ivor Court, London NW1   Paddington 3923

Of course, I had to buy every record and it took a bit of time to get the money for them but, as soon as I had them all, I telephoned and asked her if she would sign them for me. She agreed at once.

Polishing every finger mark off the sleeves I took my records to her at Ivor Court, my stomach fluttering with butterflies.

She showed me into her lounge which had a parquet floor with a couple of expensive Turkish rugs on it. The furniture was heavy oak and leather. An enormous Steinway grand piano was in the centre, draped with a shawl, and photographs of odd-looking foreigners stared impassively at me from their frames. A bookcase contained hundreds of scores, many with the titles in Russian. Painted wooden dolls stood on the mantelpiece and a sinister looking rag doll with no face lay on the couch. The cream walls held two magnificent portraits of her. One, in oils, depicted her on the recital platform, with the hair parted in the middle and pulled back, hands clasped to the bosom and the face registering the anguish about which she was obviously singing. The other portrait was in soft pastels and showed a dark-haired girl of twenty or so, innocent but with a glimmer in the eye. She had been attractive, the Slavonic eyes and cheek bones giving her an exotic look.

She was delighted when she saw all the records, and examined each one as though she had never seen it before. Mentioning their immaculate condition she told me, "When I see them like this, and it's obvious that you treasure them, then it makes everything so worth while." I replied that she must have had a marvellous career. She pursed her lips, "Not bad, I think I could have done better."

After she had signed the records I broached an idea I had been thinking about:

"Have you—" I faltered, "written your autobiography?"

"No."

"I'm surprised."

"My English is not too good. I speak French, Italian, German, Spanish, and English but none of them good, and now I am even forgetting my Russian. I cannot think in Russian and I cannot write in English." She smiled, "It is a problem, isn't it?"

"I'll help you to write a book."

"Then we will do it." Quickly as that she was sold on the idea. She seized my hand, "We will write my memoirs."

Before starting the book I wanted to hear as much as possible of her work, including some 78rpm records she told me she had made "when a girl"—in fact her first record was made when she was aged 42—and which had not been transferred on to LPs.

I found it astonishing that she did not have a record-player, for I imagined a recording artist would have the most sophisticated equipment available; but no, there was nothing.

So we arranged that I would take my portable record-player on my next visit so that we could hear her deleted and unissued records.

We started off with the Gretchaninoff "Lullaby", not the version dubbed to the Decca LXT 5663 but an earlier matrix made for HMV in 1931 and never issued commercially.

A completely different voice from the one to which I had become accustomed came from the speaker. How can I describe it? It was softer, lighter, more flexible and utterly beautiful. The top notes were petal soft and seemed to go on for ever. The "Lullaby" is meant to be sung to a baby and I remember thinking, Fancy wasting that on a child.

In later years she changed her method of production, which many considered a pity, but in this early record she didn't need to resort to any tricks, she was simply a free-flowing stream of sound. It was the young girl in the pastel portrait.

After the Gretchaninoff came Tchaikovsky's "Golden Corn-fields", which she considered the best of all her recordings, and then two or three others. But she became restless and said I must be bored by now; at any rate, she was.

When I protested she said I could do as I liked but she was going to the kitchen to make some tea. So I continued playing the records.

She seemed to be a long time so, while a record was playing, I went to see if she was all right. As I looked in the kitchen her back was towards me and her shoulders were shaking as she sobbed. I knew why instinctively and backed out without speaking. She hadn't seen me.

Although she could still sing remarkably well for her age, she had lost that fresh young voice which Richard Bebb described as the loveliest ever to come from Russia (she agreed with him, incidentally). Now, all that was left to her was a shred.

I turned off the gramophone and Slobodskaya reappeared a few moments later with a tray laden with teapot, cups, cottage cheese and cream crackers and two oranges. Her ideas on what was appropriate to eat at different meals were always varied.

She was bright and breezy, if her grief had not evaporated she disguised it well. A delicious aroma wafted from the tea as she poured her mixture of Earl Grey and Lapsang Souchong from her octagonal, art-deco teapot. I give that brief description of the teapot as it became the bane of my life and is indelibly in my memory. Much later, when I graduated to doing her washing-up I lived in terror of dropping it. Every time I laid hands on that teapot she admonished me to be careful, her glance boding the direst ill should any misfortune befall it. I once broke a cup and she never recovered from the shock. I can still feel her fist banging in the small of my back as she punched me in her fury.

But on the afternoon we first played the records, tea was free from breakages and she was in high spirits thinking about the book we would write together, and which we agreed to start the following Saturday. As I left she pressed an orange into my hand "for the journey".

For the writing sessions she had sorted out all her reminiscences, which she had put down on paper throughout the years, and which had been piled in a chaotic heap on top of the wardrobe. But the good order did not last and within days she reverted and there was chaos again. Times without number I put the papers in order again and always, sometimes within a couple of hours, she would strew them about, looking for something. When I gently taxed her she explained she didn't know how it had happened.

She had written about Prokofiev, with whom she had been a fellow student at the Petrograd Conservatoire; Glazunov, who had been the Principal; Rimsky-Korsakov, who had given lectures on opera to the students; Stravinsky, whom she actively disliked, but who gave her the chance to create the title rôle in one of his operas; Mussorgsky, her favourite composer; Shostakovitch, who had been a mere orchestra violinist when she had been a soloist; and Gretchaninoff, who had written songs especially for her.

Despite our perseverance and regular working hours it became gradually clear that our book would never be published. The number of manuscript pages did not increase beyond a certain meagre point and this was due to her habit of changing her mind about what actually had happened, and tearing up manuscript sheets which contained anything she considered prejudicial to her image. An instance springs to mind. She was in a confiding mood and talking about Fred Smith, a producer who persuaded her to record her Rimington van Wyck set:

"It is good to tell the truth," she said. "Fred knew my secret."

"What was that?"

"I was not really soprano. My voice was better suited to mezzo rôles. Fred knew this. Not that it mattered if my top C was not absolutely perfect. Who cares? I have other qualities no one else has."

I found her confession about the top C rather endearing and included it in the manuscript. When she read it, the following week, she flew into a rage:

"How dare you comment on my top C? What do you know about it? I suppose we must all bow down to you, the great voice expert? You know so much, much more than I. For your information my top C was perfect, you understand, perrfect!" She rolled the R like a lion's growl.

Before my eyes the treasured chapter of which I was so proud was snatched by her lacquer-tipped fingers and, while still ranting at me, she tore it to shreds in front of my eyes. I could only watch, mutely, as she dropped it dismissively into the waste-paper bin. And I did not utter a word of protest. In fact, I was quite contrite. It was only when I got home that I thought, How dare she.

All afternoon, comments were hurled at me. Although no one else was in the flat she addressed imaginary people, or the air. This, I came to realize, was a habit of hers: "I must be careful what I say in this flat, there is a spy with keen ears who writes everything down," or, "I thought I could speak confidentially among friends but obviously I was wrong."

After several months of work, one day she unexpectedly asked for my copy of the manuscript (we had one each). When I asked why she wanted it she snapped, "It is my property, it is my life."

I suspected something so retained the more interesting chapters and gave her the remnants.

"I thought there was more," she said.

"That's all I have," I answered. I had worked hard on that manuscript and did not want to see it go for no good reason.

I later learned that Slobodskaya had told one of her pupils to get friendly with me, get invited to my flat and then, presumably in my absence, find the missing manuscript pages and bring them back to her. Albeit she had the originals she simply did not want me to have any copies.

The reason for this became clear. She had taken the manuscript to the publishers Faber and Faber, and asked their opinion on the possibility of publishing the book as her own work. She took it as a propitious sign that Faber and Faber had agreed to read it. My copy was wanted so that I could have no possible claim to authorship.

I immediately wrote to Faber and Faber, explaining my connection with Slobodskaya and the work I had put into the manuscript. Somewhat confused, the publishers declined to have anything further to do with either of us, or our manuscript. So, after a bumpy week or two, we resumed work as usual.

On fine days Oda was prone to snap shut the exercise book in which she was writing and decide we would go for a walk. It was a decision, not an invitation. She kept all the stale crusts from her bread and these would be popped in a paper-bag so that we could feed the birds in Regent's Park. Before leaving she would examine her appearance in the hall mirrors, of which there were three arranged to give simultaneous views of front, sides and back. I waited many long minutes as she tried on hat after hat, many with veils which could be pulled over her face. More often than not she settled for her favourite Bird of Paradise arrangement. "A lady wears her hat for tea, but takes it off for dinner," she would remark, jabbing a hatpin almost through her head.

Armed with this, or similarly interesting precepts, we would leave for the park. In her bear-skin coat, scarf, gloves and feathered hat Madame was ready to face the sunshine. People might snigger when she approached but as they caught sight of her stern, asiatic face and those glinting eyes, the smiles soon faded.

The birds were duly fed which gave her much pleasure (particularly when two birds attacked each other for the same piece of bread—I'm sure she would have adored cock-fighting) and we made conversation. "I visited the graves today," she once remarked. "All my friends are dead and I shall be next." Sometimes she would sing to me and I recall a rendition of "Trees" under those same objects.

She had a friend in the park, an elderly female who slept rough, carting her possessions about in a couple of carrier bags. She catered for herself with a primus stove and saucepan, and always seemed to cook the same dish, a brownish stew she called curry. Slobodskaya and Rebecca (for that was her name) met during their mutual strolls through the park. Slobodskaya smelled the food and looked for its source. Finding it she spoke to the cook, who was cordial, and they passed the time of day:

"Do you cook like this often?" asked Slobodskaya.

"Yes, food tastes better in the open air."

"I agree with you." Oda looked meaningfully at the saucepan.

"Would you like some?"

"I would."

Rebecca would often be at her spot, and on a Saturday when we were walking, Oda chatted with her. If we coincided with her meal-time she would pass us some curry on two saucers. We were probably a bit tight-fisted with her for, although we accepted her hospitality, we never took her a present.

But do not imagine Slobodskaya frittered away all her time in the park with idle socializing and bird-feeding. She had too industrious a nature for that. I had to take a note-book and pencil and then we would settle down side by side on a bench and work on her memoirs. As soon as the mildest breeze stirred the air her hand leapt to her throat pulling her collar about her.

I asked what it had been like living in Russia during the terrible 1917 Revolution. "I loved it," she said. "It was so exciting."

She was not political. The only time I remember her talking politics was when Russia invaded Czechoslovakia in 1968. "Don't blame me," she said. "I had nothing to do with it."

She did not harbour a great love for her countrymen, and declined an invitation to a cocktail party, to which some Russians had been invited, with, "What do I want to meet Russians for? Why do you think I left?"

She summoned me to be at her flat at six o'clock one evening as her pupil, Patricia Reikes, was singing at Covent Garden and she thought we would go.

At the time I owned a scruffy little Morris Minor, with a patched hood, so when I arrived and found Oda dressed to kill in a cartwheel-sized hat, fur and jewels, I suggested it might be better if we took a taxi. But she insisted we took the car as it was "more economical" and "we are not proud", which was a double-edged compliment.

There was a problem at the outset as she would not fit into my car wearing her hat. In the end she forced herself inside, clutching the crown of the hat, and forcing her head down into her shoulders, but that did not stop it from jamming over her eyes. The fur coat became entangled with the gear stick and, as we set off, I was terrified it would rip when I changed gear.

Naturally she, who couldn't find her way along the simplest route, proceeded to give directions. She did not understand one-way streets and directed me down one, which I was too confused to notice, the wrong way. She knocked the rear-view mirror to the floor with her gesture. Scrubbing about to pick this up, the car swerved and a policeman was there to see it. He signalled for us to stop.

I did so.

The front window jammed and we had to shout through the glass. After a while he shook his head pityingly and with a Pontius Pilate indication of dismissal walked away. I was so flustered I really did not know where I was going.

Miraculously we arrived at the Opera House without further incident until I backed up to the entrance and hit the commissionaire. She was furious. "Mama Mia, you've hit him, you fool! you fool!" She emphasized her feelings, as she so often did, by hitting me. Punch after punch came at me, as I tried to avert my head. She was so strong. Meanwhile, the shaken man had dusted himself down and was opening the door for her. He waited patiently for her to stop. She must have seen something in my face for she spun round. "Forgive me," she said. "My friend drives me mad; I hope we did not hurt you?" Taking his hand she made a gracious entrance into the foyer.

Anyone who has driven to the Royal Opera House will know the hell of trying to park. It took me a long time to find a space, and when I did it was quite a distance from the theatre.

As I returned she was chatting to someone who had asked for her autograph. She hummed happily as we made our way to the auditorium. "The Queen sits here," she whispered as we snuggled into our complimentary grand-tier seats.

During the interval she was quick to stand and, as was her wont, turned full circle so that the audience could see. No one

seemed to recognize her. "Not a very musicianlly audience,"
she sniffed. In the Crush Bar she wanted a sandwich but refused
to queue so simply took one off the counter. I had to face the
angry comments and pay up. She then marched up to a little
group with an empty seat in their midst:

"Does this belong to anyone?"

"Afraid so. He's coming back in a moment."

"I'll sit here till he does."

She sat in the middle of the group, relishing her chicken
sandwich. Their conversation petered out.

Going home was murder. I left her waiting for me in the foyer
but by the time I returned with the car the Opera House was
locked up and Oda had been put into the street. To say she was
outraged is an understatement. I was greeted with a mouthful of
abuse that would have made a navvy blush, some of it was in
Russian but, by now, I knew what her Russian oaths meant. She
did not stop until I'd returned her to Ivor Court. I put her
straight into the lift, not even troubling to take her to her flat
door. She was still shouting as her feet disappeared above my head.

That was it, I decided. I'd really had enough. She had behaved
unfairly once too often. When she telephoned me in the morning,
as I knew she would, I would make it clear that I was no longer
prepared to tolerate such treatment, even if it meant jeopardizing
our relationship. I worked out exactly what I would say to her.
She would say that she expected me for lunch on Saturday and I
would reply, "After yesterday, Oda, I have decided that I have
better things to do than play nursemaid to an autocratic, selfish
eccentric. I have my own talent to offer. I shall not see you on
Saturday and shall telephone you when I am free." The telephone
call came the following morning, as expected. A Merry Widow-
type laugh came from the receiver, preceding her remarks:

"Hello darlink," she said. "Didn't we enjoy ourselves last
night?"

"You might have."

"I thought you were a little cross with me, but you understand
my temperament. I am Rrroooshan. Ha, ha."

Here it comes, I thought. And I was ready for her.

"Good, then we are friends," she continued. "We understand
each other. And I will see you tomorrow for lunch as usual?"

"Yes."

Spiritless to the end, I was there.

Another outing will never be forgotten. The wealthy mother of one of Oda's pupils hired the Wigmore Hall for the evening to enable her daughter to give a recital. Oda was obliged to attend. As the date approached she grew increasingly resentful about this intrusion on her time.

The recital was due to start at half-past seven and I was instructed to be at Ivor Court for seven o'clock. She opened the door with the, by now familiar, funereal expression on her face. She had already decided it would be an unpleasant evening:

"She is singing Hugo Wolf's Spanish Songbook," she said. "Tell me if it is one book, or two."

I looked at the programme on her table and told her one.

"Thank God. Did you see that Martinelli died?"

She took her coat from the wardrobe and I helped her on with it. No sooner was it on her back than she tore it off again:

"No, no. I will *not* be intimidated. Why should I rush? We will have tea first."

"But we've only twenty-five minutes to get there."

"So, we will be late."

Not only did we have tea, we had cake, bread and butter and biscuits. It was ten to eight by the time we set off.

As was to be expected, the foyer was deserted when we arrived, people having taken their seats quite half an hour earlier. An usher told us that there was no admission until the interval. There was a sound which, in that confined space, sounded like an explosion, as Slobodskaya threw open the auditorium doors. She decided she could not wait. Our first view was of the singer, so shaking with nerves it looked as if she had Parkinson's Disease. But every pair of eyes had been torn away from her and was now focused on the doorway.

Oda waved to a friend or two (the unlucky recipients averted embarrassed faces) and plodded down the aisle. She disturbed half a dozen people getting to our seats and all the time the singer followed our progress with unbelieving eyes, still singing. "She sounds like a cow in labour," joked Oda and had a little chuckle to herself. With that the house lights came up. It was the interval. If we had only waited a few moments longer all that commotion could have been avoided. Not that Slobodskaya was aware she had done anything untoward.

Oda's entrance was not referred to during the interval by the few who came to speak to her, but after the recital the singer's mother bore down on her, not to remonstrate, but to invite her to a party. When Oda accepted and said she had a friend with her, the woman had little alternative other than to invite me as well.

"How kind," said Oda, fluttering her fan (she often took a little circular fan to functions) and grimacing at me behind it.

Firstly, the mother said, we must collect a certain Madame Jeanne, who was also in the audience. From the back Madame Jeanne looked exquisite. Blonde hair mingled with her rich chinchilla coat, her tiny feet shod with golden shoes. From the front the effect was quite different. Something resembling saffron cement had been smeared on her face and this had been tinted pink in the cheek areas, and painted bright red around the mouth. She was incredibly old, and all her make-up couldn't disguise the terrible, dead-looking dough that was her face.

Madame Jeanne's Rolls Royce was to transport us to the party and she attempted to rise from her seat. Unaided she might have sat there till death overtook her, but Oda and I managed to hoist her to her feet and, literally, drag her to the foyer. She had a husband with her but he seemed nearly as old and feeble. Oda whispered to me that his face reminded her of the death mask of Rachmaninov.

Madame Jeanne and Oda did not take to each other and it was Jeanne's fault. While we were settling into the Rolls, not a simple manœuvre, she remarked, quite gratuitously:

"*I* was trained to be a singer, you know."

"Really?" said Oda.

"Yes, but I never sang in public, it was considered vulgar."

The party was in full swing when we arrived. During the evening the mother pointed a camera at Oda, calling for her to smile. It was dashed to the ground by Oda's fist. She did not like to be photographed in her old age and got violent if cameras were produced unexpectedly.

Some bore was enthusiastically shouting about a new production of *Oedipus* and how "a huge silver penis" was pulled on stage. Oda pretended not to hear. A magic moment occurred when she was about to reach for a glass of wine and Madame Jeanne, who had been perched nearby, seized her hand.

"Don't drink that," she said. "It's poison. All alcohol is poison, I never touch it. I drink only water."

"Perhaps that is why you stay so young," said Oda, smiling into the ancient visage and sipping her drink.

The brunt of many of Oda's attacks at Ivor Court was Smithy, her window cleaner. He was a sweet-natured, wiry man of about 50 and, really, very kind to her.

She insisted that he deliberately called to clean the windows when she was having lunch, despite her having told him several times to wait until after the lunch hour. But as her eating habits were erratic, she could be at the meal at any time between eleven-thirty and half-past three, and Smithy always seemed to catch her eating. He was always embarrassed and only too ready to apologize and beat a hasty retreat, but she wouldn't have it. Once she'd opened the door, she had decided she'd been disturbed and it would throw her into a fury. Once, she banged the table so hard when Smithy put in an appearance that the gravy slopped out of the boat. Another time Smithy was dragged in by the arm and made to wait while she set a place for him, insisting that anyone who knocked at her door at that time of day must have come for lunch.

She sat him down in his dungarees with the cloth still in his hand. There were about four of us at the table and everyone was uncomfortable. No one spoke and Smithy had to escape as best he could.

Despite this ill treatment, which could well have soured even the sweetest temperament, Smithy did all sorts of odd jobs for her.

Slobodskaya decided, one day, to have her curtains cleaned. They were heavy brocade and had not been moved for years, but in order to get them to the cleaners they would first have to be taken down. All Slobodskaya's coterie steered well clear of this job, for it was certain that as soon as the curtains were moved they would fall to pieces. It was equally certain that whoever happened to be handling them at the time would be blamed.

Poor Smithy had no option in the end. She enveigled him with bright smiles and a cup of tea, and led him like a lamb to the slaughter. He was extremely careful with the curtains but, of course, they did fall to bits. Unfortunately that was not the only disaster. To steady his balance he put his foot on the lid of her

Steinway which was raised a foot or so on its plinth. The sound as the plinth broke and the lid crashed down sounded like human bones breaking.

The scene that followed is difficult to describe: she cried, she wept, she wrung her hands and cursed Smithy, who was so contrite he was almost in tears himself.

Precious as Steinways are, window cleaners also have a certain value and, although the incident was never forgotten, she had to come to terms and talk to Smithy or suffer dirty windows. And she was not prepared to do that.

Another of his misdemeanours struck nearer her heart. Trying to placate her for something or other he pointed to the oil portrait of her and said, "I know who that is."

"Do you, Smithy," she answered, mollified.

"Oh, yes," he said. "It's Julius Caesar." What made her more annoyed was that it was a genuine mistake.

Another mistake, made in the street outside Ivor Court, could have had more serious consequences.

Slobodskaya was waiting for the bus to take her to the Guild-hall School of Music and Drama where she was teaching. Too impatient to merely wait at the stop, she would pace about and continuously walk into the road to look for the bus. On this particular occasion she stepped out into the road, without look-ing, and was hit by a car which was trying to reverse out of its parking space. It could not have been travelling more than five miles an hour but, nevertheless, it knocked her down. The doughnut-shaped hat she had been wearing rolled away a few feet and was flattened by the bus for which she had been waiting and which sped past without stopping.

The driver was out of the car in a trice, looking worried, and a couple of passers-by were helping Oda to her feet. She was crying loudly. I retrieved the flattened hat and gave it to her, which was not the most tactful thing to have done in the circumstances, but she took it without comment.

We tried to get her to sit down for a while in the foyer of Ivor Court but she insisted we return to her flat. Upstairs we had a look at the damage. She was bruised and shaken but no drastic harm done. I made her a cup of coffee which she drank, sniffing. Then she rallied round and began cursing the driver, saying it was his fault.

Within half an hour she had changed her stockings and was ready to start off for the Guildhall again. There are few ladies, not far short of 80, who could demonstrate that sort of stamina.

One of her telephone summonses reached me some time later, during which she told me she was giving a lecture-recital to some friends. Would I bring "the machine" and play some records for her?

The address she had given turned out to be the Arts Council. As she had given me to understand it was to be an informal affair, I had not troubled to arrive more than a few minutes before the appointed time. An official was waiting for me in the foyer in some agitation, and he told me that Madame was getting anxious. Hurrying me through one of the corridors I caught a glimpse of the recital room, which was replete with chandeliers and a very formally dressed audience. So much for her lecture-recital to some friends.

Slobodskaya was pacing the green room, looking magnificent in black velvet and diamanté, with a grey fur slung over her shoulders. Her eyes were glittering with fury. The general tenor of her greeting was to know where I'd been, that all her records needed to be put in order and the machine set up, that it was nearly seven and I had only just got there and that she had thought she could rely on me but now knew different. There was a lot more.

Red in the face I hastily checked that the gramophone had the correct type of plug which, thank God, it did. I had already put the records in order before setting out. All the time Slobodskaya kept nagging, telling me not to drop the records and that I had no idea of their value, that arriving late had ruined the evening anyway as she did not feel at all like singing. In fact, as always before a concert in her old age, she was terribly nervous. Behind the tirade I could hear someone on stage announcing her. While walking towards the entrance she blamed me for her foot, which hurt, and for her thin stockings, that left her legs cold, and for her back, which ached. Scowling at me she walked through the drapes on to the stage.

At the precise moment of passing through the wings an extraordinary metamorphosis took place. A wide smile instantly replaced the scowl and she nodded graciously to the applause. Gerald Wragg, her accompanist, followed and sat at the piano

Oda Slobodskaya sprawling across two pages. Just my surname was written in smaller characters underneath.

Her entrance was greeted by shouts and cries of ecstasy, which pleased her immensely. Smiling and shaking hands she just had time to slip out of her mink and toss it at me. It missed and fell to the floor. Feeling rather indignant I was inclined to leave it there and let the gesture make its own point. But, lacking the courage of my convictions, I picked it up and carefully placed it on a chair.

The scene was very Russian. A couple of balalaikas were strumming and there was much moving about, dancing and shouting. Clusters of broken glass lay on the floor. Slobodskaya took to the fray at once and ploughed straight in. "I will buy you some pampoushetski and vodka," she bellowed from across the room. And someone brought it to me. The balalaikas shrilled out a folk tune and she grabbed the nearest implement, which happened to be a spoon, and beat out the rhythm on a sugar basin. Fragments of glass shot into the air. She sang at the top of her voice, with her mouth full of food, like a kid at a party.

I wandered about and came across a stall which was selling Russian knick-knacks, so I bought a little painted wooden box for her as a thank-you present. When I gave it to her she went mad. How dare I waste money? What did she want a box for, anyway, she had at least six? It was her evening and I was not to spend my money. I was to take it back and change it at once.

I did. The lady from whom I had bought it had heard the fracas and understood. "Never mind, dear, buy the old tab a cup of tea instead."

I rejoined the old tab who was quiet for a while. Then: "I have been thinking. Perhaps I was hasty. It was nice of you to buy me a present, I think I would like the box after all."

It may seem strange for an adult man to put up with such behaviour but that was Slobodskaya's power. As her accompanist, Annette Holbron, said, "She simply had the power to make you love her." She bullied, cajoled and insulted, yet could smile, or say sorry, and everything was forgiven.

Later in the evening, when she was fondly clutching her painted box, I persuaded her to sing some English songs.

"Well, teach me some," she said.

2

So I taught her "Daisybell" which she liked, and "Don't Dilly-Dally on the Way", which was also well received.

"I remember a song I used to hear a lot during the war," she said. Perfectly positioning her voice she gave, "Yes, We Have No Bananas". It was a beautiful performance.

Now she is dead and the world is a drabber place because of it. She did not lose her vitality at all, even at the end, and even during her last, painful illness, she was making plans to return to the concert platform. It was inconceivable to Oda that the Almighty would have the impertinence to allow her to die.

She was cremated at Golders Green Crematorium in 1970.

PART TWO

Biography :

From the Marynsky to Music Hall

CHAPTER ONE

SLOWLY, AS I came to know her, her story emerged and I pieced it together bit by bit. This is her story and how she would have told it, for it is how she remembered it. All dates, performances and incidents have been verified wherever possible.

It all started in the Russian village of Vilno, near the Polish border, on 28 November 1888. In reference books her date of birth is given as 1895 but this reduces her age by seven years.

1888 was a bumper year for female singers, for it also saw the births of Lotte Lehmann, Frida Leider and Maggie Teyte.

Oda (it means poem in Russian) was the eldest of eight children, something for which she never forgave her parents. Age was always a sore point with her and, as Ivor Newton says, "a topic never to be discussed in her presence".

Being the eldest meant that she had to look after the younger children and this went against the grain, even though she did not have to do it single-handed. Her helpmates were two elderly aunts who were part of the household and they pottered about keeping a general eye on things while the parents were out at work.

Arraham Slobodski and his wife worked together in a shop which sold second-hand clothes, specializing in military uniforms which were hard-wearing and bought by the many farm workers in the neighbourhood. In later life, when Oda spoke of her father, she would explain that he was a "professional man, connected with the militia". On her marriage certificate he is described as a merchant. It was taken for granted that she, as eldest girl, would work in the shop with them when she finished school.

The family lived in rented accommodation on the top floor of an old house opposite the market square, and Oda thrived on the bustle of market days. She ran wild through the crowds, like a tomboy, and, in the evenings, when the stall-holders had left, she scoured the gutters looking for any dropped or left-over vegetables and fruit. A cauliflower was a great find as these were seldom seen and expensive, but anything was welcome. The family was not impoverished but there was not much spare cash about.

The Slobodskis were not demonstrative in their affections and did not believe in making a fuss of their children. The business of living was too serious to allow for sentiment of that kind. Oda inherited the same Spartan outlook, and it was not until she reached America that she realized some parents actually played on the floor with their children. She did not approve of the practice.

Birthdays were never celebrated, not even by a card, and at Christmas there was just a small tree with a few inexpensive presents. Yet, Slobodski did his duty, and all the children were well fed and clothed.

Oda had excellent health and an abundance of energy and, when the time came, adored going to school. She was so keen that she was often the first to arrive at the gates, which made her unpopular with the janitor who had to get out of bed to open up and let her in. How the poor chap must have dreaded the sight of the fresh-faced child banging on his door the first thing in the morning.

The tsarist school system seems to have been organized on similar lines to the existing British system. Two-tier education was available. There were the State-owned public schools where the rudiments of education were taught, which the majority of children attended, and the private schools where a fuller education could be expensively purchased. As a token of fair-mindedness a few scholarships to private schools were available to the children from the State schools, but these were hard to come by.

Oda attended a State school as an expensive education was out of the question for her parents. But she was such a model pupil, who actually asked for extra homework, that her teacher recommended she apply for a scholarship. She did, and passed, and gained admittance to a public school. Her parents were so proud that they willingly paid for the obligatory uniform.

There used to be a snapshot of Oda wearing her new uniform and she treasured this all her life, but it is lost now. She certainly looked a smart girl, all decked out in brown serge with a big, black apron and a bucket-shaped hat with a silver clasp. She spent hours polishing that clasp.

She strutted about the village like a peacock, and her brothers and sisters were dumb with admiration, as every other child they knew, naturally, went to the State school.

Despite this grandeur, she still had to mind the children after school, and often had to bath a couple of youngsters and put them to bed as soon as she got in. As a treat she would sometimes let the bigger ones stay up late to wait for their parents to come home, propping them up in their nightshirts on the old settee with their faces all scrubbed and shining. Usually they fell asleep anyway, and the Slobodskis would carry them off to bed when they got in, without waking them.

When Oda was about twelve or so she was allowed to have her evening meal with the adults. Sometimes a couple of the neighbours would call in and there would be a sing-song. Oda inherited her voice from her father's side of the family, and the aunts, his sisters, had fine soprano voices whilst he, according to Oda, was a tenor of exceptional quality who, if he had had the training, could have had an outstanding professional career.

Oda loved these sing-songs but was forbidden to join in. They were strictly for the adults and she had to stay in her corner, sitting on a cushion, and be quiet.

She was enraptured by it all and knew, too, that she had a good voice and could sing. Often on market days, when she was not at school, she would let her voice ring out, confident that the noise in the streets would drown the sound, as she was too shy to sing when others could hear her.

Sometimes she would be carried away by the songs and once her mother found her sitting on the bed, one shoe on and the other idly in her hand, singing about some legendary prince and a woman. Mother soon brought her down to earth: there were baby clothes to be washed.

There was great excitement in Vilno one day. The Tsar was travelling and his procession was expected to pass within a few miles of the village. Not that anyone would be able to see what he looked like, for, Oda maintained, the masses were forbidden to look directly at the imperial countenance. Villagers had to be content with a picture to see the face of their emperor, and these were valued as highly as the icons which hung in every house. The people were, however, allowed to watch the procession and marvel at the carriages and horseriders in their opulent livery.

So the entire community trekked to the place where the procession would pass. There were no roads, but the men took planks of wood and when the going got too rough, or the ground too marshy, these were put down to walk across. Oda, with the rest of the children, was often lifted from hand to hand above their heads.

But she saw the Tsar's procession and the memory stayed with her for ever. Despite the coronations and royal weddings, Slobodskaya considered the West had nothing to equal it.

At school Oda discovered poetry, and that she had a gift for reading aloud. She liked being on stage, and was chosen to read Pushkin to the school on his birthday, and that was a great honour, especially for a scholarship child.

Most of Oda's friends came from wealthy families, who could afford to pay for the private education; and when the time came for them to leave school and choose careers, in a dilettante sort of way, a few of them who were close to her plumped for architecture. Oda thought that she would do the same. Papa Slobodski soon scotched this, though. He was prepared to sponsor his sons' education if it was necessary, but not to squander money on a daughter. Oda had had a good schooling and that was enough. She didn't feel too bitter, it was what she had expected.

Oda first heard about opera at school, when her friends mentioned that they had seen these strange-sounding productions on visits to St Petersburg. She heard that the singers for these operas trained for years at an establishment called a conservatoire. With her love of singing she was determined to find out more. But her parents were no use, as they had never heard of such a place.

So for the present she had to be content with singing to herself, and only daring to sing without restraint when it was market day, and the madding crowd drowned the sound.

CHAPTER TWO

AFTER LEAVING SCHOOL Oda did, indeed, work in the clothes shop for a while; she was not too happy about it, feeling her education was being wasted (which, of course, it was) but there was no way out that she could see. She could have become a governess to some wealthy family, but this would have meant an upheaval as her parents would have resented a move away from home. The thought of being a governess did not inspire her anyway, and it was certainly not worth the effort of a full-scale row.

She still sang at home, and now joined in with the adults, sometimes singing duets with an aunt and sometimes folk songs by herself. In later years she was to include some of these in her concerts. There was one particular song about a gondolier that was a great favourite with the family and neighbours alike.

Old school friends still kept in touch with her and, now and then, one of these would come to visit. It was a fellow pupil who, after hearing her sing, suggested she write to the St Petersburg Conservatoire for an audition. Oda seized the idea and cursed herself for not having thought of it. She should have applied years ago, while still at school, but there had been no one to advise her. Had she been more worldly she probably would not have dared write to the conservatoire. How could she have known that most auditionees were already thoroughly schooled in music? Oda knew nothing about theory, all she had was a good voice.

Thanks to her education she could write a literate letter; an ill-written application might well have been dismissed by the board.

Sometimes when fools rush in they win through, and this was the case. She was granted an audition and told to present herself at a date several months ahead. Beside herself with excitement she was convinced she was already on the path to fame.

As the audition date approached Slobodski grudgingly gave his permission for her to attend. He thoroughly disapproved of the idea and Oda had had to choose the moment carefully to tell him. As she did not earn a salary, it meant that Slobodski would have to finance the trip to St Petersburg; Slobodski had a healthy regard for the value of money, which Oda inherited from him, and was later to practise herself.

Although it was her first trip to St Petersburg, and the distance from Vilno was about 300 miles, Oda made the journey quite alone. She was not one to be easily intimidated but, nevertheless, it must have been nerve-racking, wandering about the wide streets with their huge, elegant buildings, and seeing all the busy, smartly dressed people.

When she found the conservatoire, which must have been a feat in itself, she discovered that it was adjacent to the famous Marynsky Theatre. If she had peeped through the doors, into the auditorium, her courage might well have deserted her. For the interior of the Marynsky is among the most splendid of any theatre in the world, with its acres of turquoise plush and gilt ornamentation, and the whole thing dominated by the imperial box, starting at the first tier and rising through four levels to be climaxed by a vast, jewelled canopy. But she did not peer in and, recalling the incident later, she wrote:

The first day I crossed the Marynskaya Ploschad to the conservatoire, I did not walk, I floated. Oh, that noble square, like the Piazza de Senioria [sic] in Florence. On one side there was the solid conservatoire building and on the other the Marynsky Theatre, the pinnacle all students must strive to reach. In the middle stood a statue of Glinka.

I stepped into the corridor and was conscious of the largeness, the large wooden steps leading to the landings and the vast hall. There were parquet floors everywhere and no carpets.

I introduced myself to the attendant and asked where I should go.

She was told to wait in the corridor with some other girls. She noticed then what a bumpkin she looked, as most were well dressed and she was wrapped up in a shabby grey coat with a faded best dress underneath. Her sturdy shoes contrasted with the coloured fripperies of the other girls, who had probably had them imported from Paris. She felt self-conscious and embarrassed.

One by one the girls were called into the audition room and could be heard, through the doors, singing. It must have sounded strange to Oda, who had never heard an aria, and made her decidedly uneasy. Nowadays any conservatoire would insist on foreknowledge of the students' pieces but, according to Oda, this was not the case at the St Petersburg Conservatoire. She had not even brought music. She did not possess any and could not read it anyway.

When her turn came she was ushered into the audition room and found herself facing a panel of four adjudicators.

If she ever knew, Oda had forgotten the identity of two of these adjudicators, but the remaining two she would never forget, and they played a vital part in shaping her future. One was the director of the conservatoire, Alexander Glazunov, who achieved international fame as a composer, writing among other things eight symphonies, but is now chiefly remembered for his ballets "Raymonda" and "The Seasons". The other was Natalia Alexandrovna Iretskaya, a formidable, hard-faced autocrat whose photograph, in a black frame, was to assess all visitors to Oda's flat from its place of honour on the Steinway. She was the most famous singing teacher in Russia.

Oda felt very vulnerable as she faced this august body. There was a slight fracas at first when she told her examiners she had no music, and neither could she tell the pianist, who had agreed to improvise, in which key she sang. He had never heard of her gondolier song anyway.

She was more than a little shaken by all this, and used to say "When I think of it now I go crimson". As she sang she was acutely aware of those four pairs of eyes unsmilingly evaluating her. It was the first time she had sung before people when they had not tapped their feet, nodded to the rhythm, or at least looked as though they were enjoying it.

She need not have worried, it went well; so well that the judges were prepared to overlook her obvious musical shortcomings in favour of the quality of her voice. It could not happen nowadays, when musicianship is given greater emphasis than voice, and someone like Oda would not even be granted an audition.

When Glazunov and Iretskaya interviewed her afterwards she was staggered to learn that the singing course lasted nine years and that the fees were astronomical, and quite out of the question. That gave her a greater fright than the actual singing had done.

But Iretskaya had been impressed by her voice and had already decided that Oda would be her pupil and that she would study at the St Petersburg Conservatoire. Iretskaya brooked no argument and felled all obstacles. In response to Oda's alarmed observation that she would be almost 28 when she had finished her studies she insisted 28 was a good, solid age to start a career. As for the fees, Iretskaya had the authority to award four scholarships each year and Oda could benefit from one of these. She would also be studying under Iretskaya's personal supervision, which was an honour.

It was an honour which Oda would cheerfully have relinquished in favour of some less eminent, but less terrifying, professor. She was not at all sure she liked Madame Iretskaya.

Natalia Alexandrovna Iretskaya was a remarkable lady, and in the nine years that she taught Slobodskaya she passed on to her a technique which enabled her to sing well even when she was in her 70s. Iretskaya had been a successful singer herself, even leaving Russia to sing in the great concert halls of Europe. Although she never sang in opera, preferring to work as a soloist, she had built up an immense reputation as a concert singer. She had studied under the legendary Pauline Viardot who had also taught the famous Felia Litvinne. Viardot, with her sister Maria Malibran, had won world acclaim through her mastery of technique. Their father, also their teacher, was Manuel Garcia, a veritable Svengali who, although long dead, is still revered. Another of his pupils, Mathilde Marchesi, had been Melba's teacher. With tuition descending from such masters, and with nine years in which to study, it is not surprising that Slobodskaya gained an unshakeable technique.

Iretskaya's lover had been the pianist-composer Anton Rubinstein, the Founder in 1867 of the conservatoire, and also its first principal, and with whom she had toured. Rubinstein had greatly influenced her musical taste. He had been a pupil of Franz Liszt, and went on to become that maestro's only serious rival, possessing the same extravagant virtuosity. Yet, despite his ability, Rubinstein's work was flawed. When performing he could become the victim of a mad excitement which would mar his performances, making them uneven, even unnerving. When these fits were upon him he would sway at the keyboard and sometimes shout out in exultation. It was said that he had sold his soul to the devil and, consequently, his concerts were always full. Great a celebrity as Rubenstein was, he had always personally accompanied Iretskaya when she sang, and even wrote songs for her. One of these, "Roses", was among the first songs Oda recorded. And she did this as a tribute to Iretskaya's memory.

Iretskaya was *petite* but she had the same imperious stage manner that she bred into Oda. To acknowledge applause, Oda always gave a stiff, formal bow, never a curtsy. When presented with a bouquet she would select a single bloom and present it to the conductor. It was all part of her stage training. Iretskaya's soprano was smallish and white, but finely focused and she sang with the precision of an instrument and without a trace of vibrato. A vibrato was a criminal offence to Iretskaya and if it could not be trained out of the voice then the pupil was dismissed. A curious foible when one considers that, of all nationalities, Russian sopranos have the most pronounced and uneven vibrati. As with Iretskaya, Slobodskaya had a hatred of vibrato, and was appalled when she heard the great Spanish mezzo, Conchita Supervia, likening her voice to machine-gun fire.

After Rubinstein's death, Iretskaya had found it too dispiriting to tour, and retired as a performer, devoting her life to teaching and the social whirl of the Court circles of St Petersburg.

She lived in great style in a mansion overlooking the Neva. She spoke only French, the Court language, and pretended not to understand if a pupil was so coarse as to address her in Russian, which was considered the language of peasants. (With Oda she had had little option but to speak Russian. However, her determination to have Oda as a pupil overcame her distaste for her native tongue. Even so, she slowly, and inexorably, weaned Oda from Russian to French.)

When the Romanovs were in residence the imperial carriage would arrive at Iretskaya's mansion several times a week, and she would be taken to the Winter Palace where she would coach the Tsarina in the art of singing. Here was one pupil who was not abandoned, whatever her defects. A servant in livery walked behind Iretskaya, carrying her music in white-gloved hands. Her appointment at the conservatoire was one of distinction and had nothing to do with money.

The Slobodskis, inhabiting a more humble stratum of existence, did not have this disregard for cash, and there was considerable aggravation when Oda broke the news that she was about to study for nine years. If she had told her family she planned to travel to the moon they could not have been more stunned. To them, nine years was a preposterous amount of time to waste in study. But Oda won her case and Slobodski reluctantly gave his consent. He really had little option as Iretskaya had already decided his daughter's fate.

He later relented even more, and gave her a small allowance each term to help pay her way. In actuality, once Slobodski came to terms with the idea he quite fancied himself as the father of a budding singer. So, in 1907, Oda took her place in the St Petersburg Conservatoire and found no difficulty in adapting to the life of a student.

She needed somewhere to live and shared a room and a piano with three other girl singers. They took it in turn to practise, and the other girls played for her until she learned the rudiments of music.

The landlady was a good-natured soul who rented only to conservatoire students, so she was accustomed to the din they created. As Oda put it: "The poor dear, I don't know how she stood it. This just proves how patient Russians can be. I had many different lodgings throughout the years, and many different landladies, but this one I never forgot."

The landlady was a woman of some idiosyncrasies, addicted to cats and tobacco. There were nine felines that roamed the place at will, and God help the girl who laid a harsh hand on even a whisker. She was constantly boiling fish heads to feed them and was not over-particular about their toilet arrangements. The smell of cats' urine permeated the house and mingled with the smoke from the pound of black tobacco that she smoked each day. None of this seemed to have an adverse effect on the singers' throats.

As with all students, the girls would give parties from time to time, buying cheap vodka and lashings of the common, red caviar. Then they would dance and sing until the small hours.

It was a far cry for Oda from the insularity of Vilno and she loved it. Even the classroom was positively pleasant compared to the hard work she had had to put in at the shop. She liked studying, now there was something that was really worth the effort, with all day in which to do nothing but absorb knowledge.

Here music studies started from the beginning and this was not easy for a girl approaching twenty. Neither was it easy to suffer the stinging remarks of some of her wealthier colleagues who refused to let her forget her shop-keeper's background and made fun of her ignorance and rough clothes. But she had already had experience of this at school. Never a quitter, she was rarely too browbeaten for a swift retort and was once reported to Glazunov for calling a Polish girl a Polski, which, apparently, they do not like.

Her teacher of Harmony was a Monsieur Saccetti, who had his own ideas on how a class should be run. He liked to work in a cold room and would not allow fires even during the rigours of a Russian winter, insisting on open windows the whole time. He assured his pupils that coldness was essential for hard work. And hard work was the only road to success: "We were never to stop reading and working on harmony, we had to carry on even if we were ill in bed with a high temperature. The only time he allowed us to stop was if we were unconscious."

Sight-reading gave her great problems and she never properly mastered this. She had naturally good pitch but it was difficult to relate this to written notation. Composition was virtually impossible, and anything to do with playing the piano a strain; she never managed to play more than a few successive notes accurately.

None of this worried Iretskaya who was solely concerned with singing. Certainly it was desirable that her girls should be able to read their music, although this was not considered an essential, but she was entirely indifferent as to whether they could understand harmony or play the piano. They would never have to put either subject into practice.

All Iretskaya's pupils were trained as soloists, as she did not believe in wasting her time on future chorus ladies. When her pupils left her they were automatically leads. A recommendation from Iretskaya was good enough for any company manager or producer. The fact that she was a friend of the Tsar lent no little weight to her suggestions.

Iretskaya's training methods were severe. Those who failed to come up to expectation were soon handed down to another professor. She was slow to praise, rarely seemed pleased and could be extremely sarcastic. Her favourite disparagement of Oda was, "My dear child, whoever put the idea of a singing career into your head? There are so many other occupations for which you are better suited, why not try one?" She believed in force and had the reputation for making or breaking a voice, a method which is viewed with horror today and which Oda repudiated when she came to teach. But Iretskaya believed in forcing out the vibrato, forcing up the top notes and forcing down the chest register, whichever seemed to need the most attention. If a voice could not stand the strain, then it was not up to a professional career. Those that survived had uncrackable voices.

Oda's vocal weakness was her top register, she was rather low in tessitura for a soprano. Often, after a gruelling session with Iretskaya she would not dare use the top of her voice. Some instinct warned her she might do irreparable damage. Yet, Iretskaya definitely created some artificial top notes for her and these helped tremendously in establishing her early career, and lasted until about middle age when the voice shrank and reverted to its natural size.

Due to Oda's ignorance of theory she had to work harder than the other students to learn her exercises. She had to pick out the melody on the piano, one note at a time at first, and dare not approach Iretskaya until she had thoroughly learned the piece. Iretskaya's disregard for theory did not extend to allowing it to jeopardize her own classes, and none of her girls would be given a hearing until they knew their songs or exercises by heart.

Even when Oda became quite a mature student Iretskaya still disciplined her:

> I was dismissed from a lesson because I could not give Iretskaya an accurate translation of "Ah! perfido". I left the room crying bitterly and clutching the dictionary I had been given to study. But it taught me a lesson for the rest of my life. Never again did I go to a class without thoroughly knowing my words.

Fortunately for the girls Iretskaya did not believe in early rising, and her classes did not begin until eleven in the morning. But only a fool would arrive even a few seconds late. She would tell the latecomer: "I am an old lady yet I get here on time but a young girl like you cannot manage. Perhaps you had better not bother at all." And the lesson would be cancelled for the day.

The first part of any stature that Oda studied at the conservatoire was the Angel in Tchaikovsky's *Jeanne d'Arc*. The following passage indicates how seriously she took her art, and it also shows a leading lady in the making:

The voice of the Angel guides Jeanne to save her people. This is the voice which inspired Jeanne on her mission and led her to the bitter end, it gave her conviction and courage.

None of the girls at rehearsal had heard me sing and, when I opened my mouth, I suppose it was a surprise to them. But I was unconcerned with them, all I thought of was my intonation. When I had finished they did not speak to me, and gathered in little groups talking. I took it as a bad sign. Probably I was a little sharp on the high notes. I was so depressed I would not see anyone for a couple of days. I just did my lessons, attended rehearsals and went home alone. I even went to the canteen at a time I thought not many people would be there, so that I wouldn't be embarrassed by the stares.

I was sitting there one morning when a girl sat opposite me and started to talk about *Jeanne d'Arc*. She told me, "We all knew you had a fine voice but we didn't expect such *expressive* singing."

I realized that the conspiracy had been about the good impression I had created and the silly young things had not come to me and comforted me with a good word, a word of praise, which would have sent me straight to heaven.

The whole conservatoire loved Glazunov. With his courtly clothes and kindly manner, even Madame Iretskaya had a soft spot for him. He was not forbidding and encouraged all the students to go directly to him with their troubles. He even gave them money at times, if they were having difficulties making

ends meet, and this always came from his private income. Because
of his kindness, Glazunov's indisposition was overlooked. He
had fits of manic depression coupled with alcoholism. When the
fit was upon him he would lock himself up in his study, with his
servant carrying up bottle after bottle. He would refuse to eat or
to see anyone. Then, when the sickness had passed, he would
return to his duties and things would continue as normal.

It was entirely due to Glazunov's good offices that Oda was
not expelled from the conservatoire. Iretskaya refused to allow her
girls to sing small professional rôles during their training. Some
of her students were resentful about this as they could have put
the money they would have earned to good use.

Despite her father's small allowance, Oda was always desperately short of money, and when she heard that the Marynsky
needed chorus singers she could not resist the temptation and
joined the company. For a while she was undetected and put the
money to good use. Then, one ghastly evening, a performance of
Parsifal was given in the presence of the imperial family. As tutor
to the Tsarina, Iretskaya was invited by the Tsar, Nicholas II,
to join the royal family in their box. That night Oda was cast as
a flower maiden and Iretskaya had an uninterrupted view of her
on stage. Oda had no idea Iretskaya was in the royal box as she
made her curtsy to the Tsar with the rest of the supporting
players at the end of the performance. It was as well the foot-
lights masked the barrage of fury emanating from her professor,
or she would not have slept at all well that night.

Much was said the next morning and Iretskaya refused to
continue to teach her "ungrateful pupil" and demanded her
expulsion from the conservatoire. Nothing Oda said could
dissuade her, not the years of study, her glowing prospects,
nothing. Iretskaya had been defied, it was heresy. When Glazunov
called for Oda to account for herself and learned of her money
problems, instead of expelling her he made her a personal
allowance. He then spoke to Iretskaya and calmed her, gradually
persuading her to reverse her decision and to continue to teach
Oda. So Oda had to make a full, public apology, and slowly
reinstated herself with Iretskaya.

The next time Oda disgraced herself Iretskaya was even more
loath to forgive, although she had not been directly disobeyed
and, consequently, did not demand expulsion. Oda had graduated

to singing leading rôles in student productions and these were given in front of an audience, at the conservatoire.

I was singing Aida and Prokofiev was the conductor. I thought I was the great prima donna but I made a mistake and came in too early. Prokofiev signalled for me to stop but I would not. I was the soloist, let the others stop, not me.

I carried on singing and again, this time more urgently, Prokofiev signalled for me to stop, but still I would not.

When the ensemble came in it was a disaster. Prokofiev was furious and broke his baton in two and strode away.

Iretskaya was disgraced by me and her punishment was to restrict my lessons to the very minimum, just ten minutes or so. Previously I had been one of her favourite pupils, accustomed to long lessons. From the top of the tree I found myself at the bottom, and I stayed there for a long time.

A heavy depression came on me which lasted for weeks and would not leave. Whatever I sang or did was treated with indifference. Iretskaya would not even speak to me, my humiliation was too painful to describe. Even the other girls got over their fury and remarked how badly she was treating me, but I had to put up with it. I was studying under Iretskaya, that was all.

In those days one did not leave as soon as something went wrong and I persevered with my lessons as much as ever. I would go to Iretskaya, sing and leave, she sitting at the piano, grim and unmoved. She no longer showed any interest in my singing. I, too, lost courage and felt restricted. But I worked twice as hard to try to please her.

After a long time with no change in her attitude, I brought her "Pleurez, mes yeux" from Massenet's *Le Cid*. It suited my voice and seemed to express exactly how I felt. When I finished the recitative I felt like crying and my throat hurt, but I didn't cry, I continued with the aria and meant every note I sang.

When I finished, expecting the customary silence, I collected my music and went to leave. She didn't look at me, she just examined her fingernails and nonchalantly said, "You're improving, it seems you have some talent, after all."

This was the greatest compliment she had ever paid me. Previously, if I had excelled myself she might say, "Well, you tried, that was sincere." It was too much for me in my state of downfall. I broke down completely and cried my heart out.

Iretskaya put her hand on my shoulder to stop me and then, in compassion, she put her little arms round me, saying, "Cry, Slobodskaya, cry, it is good to cry. You know, only through tears can true art be achieved." And, you know, she was right.

CHAPTER THREE

IN ODA'S DAY it was the policy of the Marynsky Theatre to fill vacancies in their roster with conservatoire students. This meant that, in certain instances, a student could walk straight from the classroom into a leading rôle. This is what happened to Oda.

Iretskaya, as may be expected, was instrumental in arranging this. After Slobodskaya had vindicated herself with "Pleurez, mes yeux", Iretskaya arranged for her to sing the leading rôle of Tamara in a conservatoire production of her beloved Rubinstein's *The Demon*. After this, acclaim was heaped on both their heads and Iretskaya knew that her pupil was now ready for the Marynsky. As Iretskaya served on the Board of Directors there was no great difficulty in arranging the début. Another factor in Slobodskaya's favour was that the Marynsky's distinguished Wagnerian tenor, Ivan Ershov, had taken a decided fancy to her, and although he was twenty years her senior, the two were frequently seen together both in and out of the conservatoire. Ershov was also on the Board of Directors.

Oda did not suffer greatly from nerves when the date was announced. It was now 1916 and during her nine years of study she had frequently been back-stage at the Marynsky, so she knew the artists and stage hands well, and it was no more than she expected. After all, Iretskaya only trained leading ladies. The opera chosen for her début was Tchaikovsky's *Pique Dame*, and Slobodskaya was to sing the leading rôle of Lisa, opposite Ershov. Iretskaya personally coached her. In those early days she had a tremendous confidence:

If someone mentioned an aria was difficult I would say "Not for me". It was not that I was vain, I was always quiet and modest, but I knew my voice came directly from God. No one had what I had. I did not say too much to the other students but I knew none of them had a voice like mine.

It was a foregone conclusion that *Pique Dame* would enjoy the success it did, and it was the first of many rôles she was to sing at the Marynsky in a career which spanned five years. Included in her repertoire were Elisabeth de Valois, Aida, Sieglinde, and Tatiana in *Eugene Onegin*.

Great as was Oda's success, Russia in 1916 had grimmer things to think about. Within a year the revolution had broken out, which was a year later to throw the country into a state of civil war. In Petrograd (St Petersburg was renamed in 1914) during the winter of 1917/1918 there was little food, no heating to offset the bitter cold, and insufficient and inadequate clothing. Someone who was in Russia at the time and remembers the situation vividly is the conductor Anatole Fistoulari:

> Life was incredibly difficult. It was freezing and everyone was half-starved. My father managed to get some food for us one day which turned out to be a piece of rotting meat, which he brought home in a sack. To us it was a feast and we were tremendously excited. But it gave us typhoid.
>
> We tried to live our lives and continue with our careers but it was difficult to move about as transport was totally unorganized. We never knew who was running the country or which particular faction was in power.

Oda admitted she fared better than most for, she explained, as a singer, she was allowed to maintain her strength with a daily ration of two ounces of bread, and her comparatively high salary allowed her to buy food on the flourishing black market.

The people of Petrograd still tried to lead a life as near the norm as possible and continued to attend theatres and the opera house. Oda did not attempt to understand the political situation and sang for whichever side happened to hold power at the time. When detailed to do so, she took leave from the Marynsky and joined the bands of singers who were ordered to travel to the farms and factories and entertain the workers. For these tours Oda travelled with the rest of the company in the back of a lorry.

In her old age, Oda would tell enquirers that she loved the revolution as it was exciting. This was just for effect. She could hardly have loved seeing one of her brothers being beaten up by a mob, which she claimed happened, while she had to be held back by friends screaming for help which did not arrive.

Once she was persuaded by fellow artists to attend an illegal political meeting held in a wood just outside Petrograd. A group was gathered to discuss tactics but was broken up by the arrival of a rival group. Fierce fighting ensued and several were wounded, some killed. Oda ran, she ran for miles in panic. It was the last political meeting she attended, and it took her months to get over the shock.

Iretskaya fared badly in the revolution, and was stripped of position and property. She ended her days sharing a small, squalid room with no heating, no light and, after a short time, little furniture as she had burned most of the expendable items to keep warm. She slept on the floor. Her students did what they could for her, bringing oddments of clothing and food. But what nourishment could they provide from a city near to starvation? Oda never did discover what ultimately happened to her.

It was during one of Oda's prescribed tours that she met Chaliapine. Although never liking him she worked with him on many subsequent occasions and acknowledged he was a genius, "jeanoos" as she used to pronounce it. Oda frequently said that she thought Chaliapine the meanest man in the world, and told how he hoarded all the small luxuries that, being such a celebrity, sometimes came his way. He would not share these perks with the rest of the cast. Another thing that rankled her was that he was the only member of the company who could charge for his autograph, and, despite this, still get asked. Her dislike was suppressed though, as he was a fierce man and frightened her. He also had sufficient influence to remove from the company anyone whom he did not like.

Even so the great Chaliapine had to tour the factories in a lorry, like anyone else, and one journey that Slobodskaya and Chaliapine shared turned into a nightmare; but it had nothing to do with a clash of temperaments.

The lorry in which they were travelling got stuck in a rut and the driver ordered everybody out and tried to free the wheel with a jack. As he was trying to raise the wheel the jack slipped and the lorry crashed on to his chest, breaking the jack and pinning him to the ground. The artists tried frantically to lift the wheel but it couldn't be budged. Even Chaliapine, a giant of a man, could do nothing. And all the time the driver screamed in agony; the more they tried to help the more pain they brought him. He begged someone to shoot him as he couldn't bear the torment, and, eventually, one of the tenors, who could stand the screams no longer, shot him through the head.

Other trips were less dramatic. The workers were highly appreciative of the concerts but could not pay the artists in money so gave them value in kind. For one performance Oda received a bale of white cloth, out of which she could make clothes, and Chaliapine was given enough astrakhan fur to make a luxurious collar for his coat. Somewhere else Oda was given a sack of oats for which she was supremely ungrateful, remarking tartly, "Did they think I was a horse?" Even in starvation times she refused to eat oats, they might scratch her throat.

As all the buildings were unheated, the Marynsky stage, with its vast expanse, was absolutely freezing. She had to wear long, woollen underwear under costumes to be able to sing at all. Sieglinde was her most dreaded rôle as, during the action, she had to lie immobile on stage for a long time. She longed for her cue just to be able to move and restore the circulation.

Ironically, Oda would explain, it was the revolution that gave her one of her biggest breaks. That and the particular topography of Petrograd. The story was as follows.

It is a city full of rivers which, at that time, had to be crossed by drawbridges, which were retracted at night to allow the river traffic to pass to the sea. When up, the bridges prevented the inhabitants of one side of the city from getting to the other, a useful device in times of riot.

During a particular performance of *Don Carlos*, starring Chaliapine, which was to be held at the Norodny Dom, the Bolsheviks decided to storm the Dom and stop the performance.

The authorities learned of this intention, and hoisted up the drawbridges, foiling the attack.

Unfortunately the soprano who was to sing Elisabeth de Valois was also stopped, as she was not yet at the Dom and trapped on the wrong side of the river.

I lived on the same side as the Dom, and was sent an SOS to come and sing. I was delighted, as it was a prestigious event, and arrived as soon as I could. Having no costume I had to make do with bits and pieces borrowed from the chorus, and it was difficult to find a pair of shoes to fit me. In the end I settled for a long skirt and woollen socks on my feet, it had to do. By the time all this was done the curtain was an hour late in rising.

Oda leaves many things unexplained in this account, but, accepting that it is vested in reality, it says a lot for her steady nerves that she got through the performance at all. Chaliapine was not over helpful either, as he was put out, both at having to wait an hour for the curtain to rise and at singing with a soprano with whom he had not rehearsed. He added nothing in the way of reassurance and this, more than anything, unnerved her. According to Slobodskaya's account, at one point when Chaliapine, as Philip II of Spain, orders Elisabeth de Valois from his presence, she took one look into his fiery eyes and fled with genuine terror into the wings. She was later complimented on this realistic piece of acting.

After the opera she was treated with great civility by the management as, without her, there could have been no performance. And from then on she regularly sang at the Norodny Dom with Chaliapine. Which meant that despite the fierce look Chaliapine had not been displeased by her singing.

After the civil war of 1918–1920, apart from a few influential persons, it was forbidden to leave Russia without special permission, and this was rarely granted. One or two of Oda's colleagues had slipped out of the country and defected to Western Europe, and rumours began to filter through of the wide acclaim singers received there, and of their inflated salaries. This was the era when Melba and Butt toured in their private railway carriages with monogrammed sheets, and servants. It was all fantasy to Oda but she became increasingly dissatisfied with conditions in Russia and realized that there must be more to life than austerity and terrorism. Somewhere there was a place of freedom and plenty and she wanted to go there. Accordingly she made her plans to escape.

She dare not confide in anyone, not even her family, but after much scheming her strategy was complete. God knows how she had the courage, or who helped her, but with a pathetic bundle of possessions, including the white cloth she had been given, food, a bottle of water and a blanket, she stowed away aboard a cattle train bound for Berlin. Her travelling companions were eight horses and this was a bonus, as the heat from their bodies helped to keep her warm. Hiding in the straw, this was her home for eight days. Who knows how she managed for fresh water and food, after her pathetic supplies ran out. Or how she hid herself from the officials at the borders. But she arrived, intact, in Berlin and threw herself on the mercy of the Germans, and they did not send her back.

Later, Oda was to have her furs and her diamonds, but no one could say she had not earned them.

CHAPTER FOUR

IN BERLIN ODA made friends with the Russian ballerina Preobrajenska, who had left the Soviet Union in 1921, and moved in with her until she could establish herself. The dancer introduced her to her agent, "a remarkable woman named Louise Wolff" as Oda used to say. Although Oda was unaware of it, Miss Wolff was one of Europe's foremost concert agents. This was Oda's first experience of a theatrical agent, but she quickly realized that the breed would be of use to her. Oda sang for Miss Wolff in her office, and was accepted as a client. Miss Wolff then arranged for her to take part in a recital.

Slobodskaya's Berlin début was at the Beethovensaal. A few of the critics covered the occasion but she had to have their reviews translated as she spoke only a few words in German. The following is translated from the *Wossische Zietung*, written early in 1922:

> What shall we say about this artist who is a singer by the grace of God? Shall we say she has an exceptionally beautiful voice in point of softness and tone? That her diction is perfect and her knowledge of putting forth her vocal gifts extraordinary? That her musical instinct prompts her to sing the natural musical phrase and that her inborn temperament lifts her to the highest pathos? That, on the whole, the impression you receive is one of artistic completeness and perfection? All these things could be said about her, her reception was a triumph and we can only hope that her enforced stay abroad will acquire for her the European fame she deserves.

Louise Wolff arranged a follow-up concert and invited the Russian impresario Max Rabinoff. In his day Rabinoff was a top operator, who had launched Pavlova on her career. Few remember him now, but Dame Alicia Markova recently spoke of his "great personal charm and powers of persuasion". Rabinoff

had called on Markova in New York and tried to convince her
she should sign up with him, although she was already represented by Sol Hurok. He failed with Dame Alicia but Oda did
not have Sol Hurok and was more than willing to be persuaded
by Rabinoff that he should be her personal manager. Oda spoke
of Rabinoff as "audacious, big thinking and with magnetic eyes".
It seemed she was smitten by him.

Rabinoff suggested she join the principals in a new company
he was forming to tour America. This threw her into a quandary,
one of the many which beset her. Never among the most decisive
people over business matters, as much as she wanted to be
represented by Rabinoff, she also wanted to go to Italy and
audition for Toscanini. Everyone she knew, and by now the
circle had widened, had to give an opinion. The advantages of
going to America were obvious, but having just arrived in
Western Europe it seemed absurd to leave before trying for
openings in opera. Particularly after just two recitals, when few
had had the opportunity of hearing her.

It was Diaghileff who solved her problem. He had heard of her
arrival in Berlin and sent a telegram from Paris, asking her to
audition for the leading rôle in a new Stravinsky opera *Mavra*
which he was presenting at the Opéra and which would be
conducted by the illustrious Gregor Fitelberg. Now there were
no doubts. She must go to Paris. Diaghileff was the greatest
impresario in the world and had moulded the careers of Fokine,
Nijinsky, Stravinsky and many others. A request from
Diaghileff was like a royal command, to refuse him would have
been artistic suicide.

Oda caught the train to Paris and presented herself to
Diaghileff, whom she described as "a fat man with a monocle
and a florid buttonhole". That seems to have been her most
durable impression of him. He took her to meet Stravinsky who
explained that *Mavra* was a one-Act opera-buffo based on
Pushkin's poem "The Little House at Kolemna". The plot
concerns Parasha who replaces her mother's cook with her lover
disguised as a girl, and who has to make his escape when discovered shaving.

Slobodskaya did not have a great deal to do with Diaghileft
who, after hearing her sing and engaging her, seemed to keep
his distance. A hint as to why this happened was given by

Slobodskaya when asked whether Diaghileff was demanding. She snapped, "Not with me. No one told Oda what to do. I had the reputation for being a little difficult. If I didn't like a thing then I didn't do it." The conformist style of the Marynsky had clearly had no lasting effect on her character and she was never over imbued with *esprit de corps*.

Stravinsky could not be so easily brushed aside, and she was working directly with him. *Mavra* was Slobodskaya's first experience of modern music and she did not like it. At that time she was the most traditional of singers and the new musical frontiers which Stravinsky was extending did not inspire her, rather it had the reverse effect. She was accustomed to having proper breathing spaces in her music, and adhering to a tempo that was consecutive for more than half a dozen bars at a time. She also liked melody. Stravinsky beat down these conventions with an iron fist and his noisy orchestration for *Mavra* consisted of clarinets, trombones, trumpets and tuba and the whole work was influenced by the jazz mania which was sweeping the world. Slobodskaya had to snatch her breaths where she could, follow the notes slavishly, and lock her eyes on to the conductor to get the constantly fluctuating timing. There was little melody and no time for a ravishing tone, just the ever-onward rush.

Once rehearsals got down to basics Oda gave Stravinsky her opinion of his revolutionary new work. She did not say what he replied but, ever afterwards, she could not hold a conversation in which Stravinsky was mentioned without referring to him as "that brute".

Stravinsky often accompanied her during rehearsals and was adamant about how he wanted things done. And he had the full support of Diaghileff who was financing the project. Although she later sang many of his songs, Slobodskaya did not work with Stravinsky, or Diaghileff for that matter, after *Mavra*.

The fine, white material that Oda had brought from Russia travelled everywhere with her for, as soon as she had the money, she wanted to have it tailored into a stylish coat. With her fee for *Mavra* she could now do this, so she hired a top couturier and was delighted when, some days later, the finished garment arrived. It had a nipped-in waist, flared sleeves and huge, military-style cuffs and, as far as she was concerned, was pure heaven. As soon as it arrived she started to wear it, and it was hanging in her wardrobe when she died. It was a treasured possession and, after each wearing, was carefully brushed, put on a hanger and wrapped in tissue paper. Oda was never careless and every cardigan, blouse or skirt was folded and put away immediately after use. She took such care of her clothes that, for many years, she managed with just two stage dresses, the eau-de-nil and another in flame lamé.

The white coat was worn for all the rehearsals and she refused to take it off, even for a moment, no matter how warm the weather. The reason for this was simple. Her dress beneath did not match up to it. After she had worn the coat for a few days some kind member of the company informed her that black was the colour that year and no respectable lady of fashion would be seen dead in white. A piece of advice she sensibly disregarded.

The Parisians loved *Mavra* and its première on 2 June 1922 was spectacular. Diaghileff invited all his influential friends, among whom were Isadora Duncan and Ernest Ansermet, and Slobodskaya had the thrill of seeing her name printed on the score. A copy of that score was another of her treasured possessions. Another pleasant thing about *Mavra* was that it reunited her with one of Iretskaya's old pupils, whom she had known at the conservatoire, the Russian mezzo Sadoven, who sang a different repertoire so could not be considered a rival. Oda was fond of her and together they explored Paris and Oda fell in love with the city. She always enjoyed a good meal and it was partly through the food that Paris reached her heart:

> I adjusted myself immediately to the French cuisine, the quality of the cooking appealed to my taste. I had my first oysters in Paris and took to them at once.
>
> It was delightful to stay in a nice hotel and have my breakfast brought up to me in bed, those marvellous large beds with linen sheets.
>
> I could smell that special smell of Paris when the streets are first flushed with water from the truck which lays the dust. And the sunshine was warm, not too hot. I thought I was in Paradise.

Although the city was marvellous she was resentful about the sophisticated social life:

Those luxurious dresses women wore to go to theatres or concerts! Every woman I met was struggling to look chic at any cost, and usually getting a private couturier to copy original models.

Most model dresses were created for *petite* people and when I tried them on they were never my size, not that I could have afforded them anyway, the prices were quite beyond me. All I could do was look and pretend to be a customer and hope that the assistants would not bother me.

A woman was always well treated when she was with a man as that meant she was a real customer because the man would pay the bill. But I was not with a man. Poor me, I was lost, I usually came out of the shops with lovely ideas but no purchases. It did not look as though I would ever have any decent suits or dresses at those prices. My great desire was to have beautiful evening gowns for my concerts but it was a long time before I could afford such luxuries.

I did not like the idea, then so prevalent in Paris, that every successful woman must have a lover, even if he is a dried-up old man. In Paris a woman's prestige is low if she is alone, and I was in this category. I felt that my social standing did not match my artistic status. The latter I carried with pride and assurance but at the same time very humbly—too humbly to utilize the advantages I held over that masqueraded, artificial way of life. I like naturalness and dislike anything artificial in people.

After *Mavra* Oda returned to Berlin and found Rabinoff still waiting for her, and just as keen to take her to America. By now he had a name for his company, The Ukranian Chorus. This consisted of a large choir, supported by four soloists, and the repertoire was to be exclusively Russian.

After the success of *Mavra* Oda felt more secure and aware of her value. She felt she could afford to be impulsive if she so desired, and a couple of months touring America with Rabinoff seemed highly desirable. She signed the contract. He sailed before her to arrange the bookings etc. and, as he was now to be her personal manager, arranged her American début: a solo concert at Carnegie Hall, to be preceded by wide publicity and a recording session.

Before leaving, Rabinoff gave Oda a first-class ticket for the *Mauretania* which was to sail from Cherbourg to New York a few weeks later. She had plenty of time in which to get ready but, incredibly, missed the boat. She arrived on the quayside in time to see it steaming towards the horizon. Almost every official at the port was included in her rage.

Her delay was caused by some last-minute insecurity concerning her documentation. She was frightened that her papers might not be in order and she might be sent back to Russia. On the morning of the crossing she was sitting in the American Consulate's office checking that every detail was in order. Her worry is understandable but not so understandable is that she waited until the day of the voyage before doing anything about it.

When Rabinoff received her cable telling how she had missed the boat he was furious. He had already arranged for a press reception in the VIP lounge at New York, which would provide some of the all-important publicity for her Carnegie Hall début. Because of her mismanagement it had to be cancelled which meant not only the loss of the publicity, but the rupturing of good relations with the press, a vital ingredient in the life of any impresario. In his fury Rabinoff cancelled Slobodskaya's recording sessions and gave them to another singer. Which is a contributory reason why there are so few recordings of Slobodskaya in her prime.

CHAPTER FIVE

ODA EVENTUALLY ARRIVED in New York on the less
prestigious liner *Coronia*, and made her peace with Rabinoff.
Fortunately she was still in time for her Carnegie Hall début.
Although conciliatory to Rabinoff she wasn't at all contrite in
her heart: "If it happened now," she said when she was in her
70s, "I would be upset but at that time I did not realize what
commitments meant in the life of a so-called artist. I was giddy,
sans souci."

Neither was she intimidated by the thought of braving
Carnegie Hall: "I was not worried, I knew I could do it and that
my voice would not let me down. It was not vanity, simply
accurate self-appraisal."

While crossing the Atlantic she made friends with some of the
other passengers and one of these had suggested what she should
wear for her début. Someone who obviously knew nothing about
it, and advised an unpretentious black dress. Oda used to explode
whenever she thought back on it: "Unpretentious for a début,
how ridiculous! And for America of all places! To think I went
on stage in a miserable little black dress. If I knew then what I
know today I would have worn my most exotic gown."

Despite the dress, the début was successful and she made her
mark on New York. Rabinoff treated her well and installed her in
the exclusive Majestic Hotel. With this as her base she enjoyed
Manhattan:

> I felt grand in my new surroundings with every comfort
> straight after the Marynsky Theatre where there was a struggle
> for mere existence. Well, Oda was being treated like a real
> prima donna and she must live up to it. But how to put on
> airs? It is not in my nature or capabilities.

She learned.

Rabinoff had engaged only the best performers for The

3

Ukranian Chorus; the chorus was excellent and the conductor was Alexander Koshetz. Another of the principals was his niece, the soprano Nina Koshetz, who had left Russia a year previous to Slobodskaya, and whose recordings are now so hotly pursued by collectors. * Strangely the two sopranos hit it off, perhaps because of the bond of their mutual exile from Russia. Although Oda, who disapproved of alcohol, could hardly have felt at ease with Madame Koshetz's drinking habits. Koshetz was quoted by *Newsweek* magazine on 28 February 1949, as saying, "What do I drink? I drink everything but gasoline, and you can quote me on that!"

It was with a feeling of sadness that Oda left New York to start The Ukranian Chorus tour. She had made friends there and it seemed a shame to leave so soon after she had settled down. She never really liked touring and this one was scheduled to last at least a year. Perhaps she had some foreboding of what was going to happen.

The Ukranian Chorus was artistically sound and praised by the critics but the public did not respond and audiences were sparse. Within a short time Rabinoff was in deep financial trouble. Oda sensed that the unrelieved diet of Russian music lacked appeal, and pleaded with Rabinoff to allow her to include some popular Italian arias but he would not hear of it, determined his programme would remain exclusively Russian. Rabinoff was a tough and experienced fighter and was not giving up without a struggle. He tried every trick he knew to keep the Chorus alive and when these failed invested his own capital.

In Tampico, Mexico, the concert was held in a bullring. Oda again tried to persuade Rabinoff to allow her to include some popular tunes. By now he had been worn down by failure so agreed to a compromise. If there was a demand for an encore she could sing just one Italian aria. She already knew what she wanted and, with Alexander Koshetz's help, arranged the details. She wrote about it in her diary:

What a tremendous experience when, at the end of the evening,

---

*Until recently recordings of Nina Koshetz were exceedingly rare but in 1978 an LP was issued by International Piano Archives (IPA 116) of Madame Koshetz singing songs by Rachmaninov, Tchaikovsky, Arensky and Sadero. Most of the record is devoted to Rachmaninov by whom Madame Koshetz was personally coached in these songs. She sets high standards and the recording is unreservedly recommended to all devotees of refined, expressive bel canto.

I sang "Vissi d'arte". The temperament of the Mexicans brought a new touch to my reception and primitive, unrestrained applause burst about me like a storm.

They cheered and shouted as though they would never stop, flinging their sombreros into the air and on to the stage. Those that wore button-holes threw them as well. I had never experienced anything quite like it before.

Doubtless that cheered up Mexico for her. Also in her diary she recorded her impressions of Mexico City:

I was staying in a most comfortable hotel and there was a military barracks nearby. Each morning I was awakened by the sound of trumpets calling the reveille from the barracks. This was a new sound to me as I was more accustomed to Russian church bells but I found the trumpets invigorating and grew to love them.

But there was another side of Mexico City which did not bring me so much happiness. The poor people, the unfortunates, sleeping on the pavements in blankets, huddled together to keep warm. This was the sad part of the city.

There were beggars all the time and the poor people stretched out their hands to me, asking for money. It was enough to break my heart.

I felt the conditions in which I was living left too great a gap in this society. One feels guilt but what can be done about it? I tried to put myself in their position and remorse would overcome me.

But life is what it is. I made myself forget the unpleasant pictures and enjoyed my work and comfort, meeting well-fed people in happy circumstances. One cannot change the injustices of the world.

Even with the success of "Vissi d'arte" Rabinoff refused to accede to popular taste. Consequently he could not fill the halls and The Ukranian Chorus had to be abandoned with an appalling financial loss. This left Oda in a precarious state as Rabinoff could not pay her. But it did not seem to alter her affection for him: "In America, where money matters so much, it was refreshing to be with a man who placed artistry above financial success."

Oda had the choice of returning to Europe and auditioning for Toscanini and other important conductors or staying in America and trying for the Metropolitan Opera House in New York, and other opera houses and recital halls. As Rabinoff was staying in America she decided to do the same. So she moved back to New York.

This time, however, she did not stay at the Majestic. As she now had to pay for her own board she settled for a modest establishment for ladies called the Park Hotel.

Oda could be thrifty so she managed to spread what money she had over a long period. But this time New York was not as joyful for her. With Rabinoff concentrating on paying off his debts he could not mastermind her career. She had never had to look for bookings and had no idea how to set about it.

She enrolled with an agency but no one seemed interested and there were no engagements. The fact that she had been part of a failed tour did nothing to enhance her. She was just another out-of-work singer. There was nothing to do but invest what little remained of her money in a couple of concerts. But she had to take small halls, and could not afford to advertise properly, so she lost her savings.

CHAPTER SIX

AFTER THE FAILURE of Oda's self-sponsored concerts she did not sing in public for a couple of years.

She was contemplating returning to Europe and Louise Wolff, who would surely have forwarded her fare and found her work, but failure leaves a bitter taste and she did not want to face her German friends and confess she had been idle for so long.

This did not prevent her from being insulted when Rabinoff came to her with a new proposition. She flatly turned him down and would not even discuss the matter. It was his turn to persevere and, when he agreed she could use an assumed name, she reluctantly, very reluctantly, said yes. The money would be extremely useful and it was only for one week in Baltimore, where no one knew her. She could do the job, pocket the money, and no one would be any the wiser.

Rabinoff was too much of a fighter to remain inactive for long. The public had beaten him down because he would not pander to its taste for the vulgar. He would beat the public at its own game. Oda had had great success with the popular "Vissi d'arte", why shouldn't she repeat this? This time in a different environment, not a new production of *Tosca* or a concert hall, but a Variety theatre.

With her strictly classical training Slobodskaya nearly had a fit when Rabinoff made his suggestion. While in America, she had seen Variety and considered it beneath her with ". . . the horrible red-nosed comedians and the stupid soubrettes".

Odali Careno was to be her Variety name. Odali as it was similar to Oda, and Careno after the famous classical pianist. That made her feel she wasn't letting the side down too badly. She also insisted on singing classical arias, no ballads or popular songs.

Full of dread she travelled to Baltimore for the first band call of her life. With the money for the engagement she bought a new dress, a complicated "eau-de-nil" arrangement in satin which

was tight to her figure with a floating panel at the back. It was as
well that it was expertly made as she wore it for the next 40
years.

Her début in Music Hall was in 1928, and she was just 40 years
old. The *Baltimore Evening Sun* covered the occasion:

> Out of Russia, that land of romance and revolution, came a
> singer of such unusual quality, of such splendid voice and
> marvellous technique as to sway to her will even the least
> interested of vaudeville.
>
> Nothing has better demonstrated the fact that the public
> always recognize true genius, than the reception accorded
> Madame Careno.
>
> Wonderingly they stared at the tall figure in its stately
> yellow gown, as she swept on to the stage with inimitable
> manner. Wonderingly they reached for programs to inquire
> into the meaning of this strange apparition.
>
> She is the luxuriant prima donna, steeped in temperament
> and exotic manner. In addition to this she really can sing.

The reviewer merely echoed the general consensus, she was a
hit. Management, Rabinoff and Oda were all delighted. No one
had expected such a sensation. Her engagement was extended for
another week.

During that week, which was equally successful, she had
business conferences with Rabinoff and a representative from the
wealthy Keith Circuit, which owned theatres in every state in
America and Canada. The outcome was that she would immediately start a coast-to-coast tour.

Within a short time she had perfected her act and began to
enjoy her new position as a Variety queen: "I took to being a
star, it suited me. I liked it when the commissionaire would
touch his cap and say 'Good evening, Madame Careno,' even
though he had never seen me before."

She enjoyed a great deal of publicity and radio broadcasts but
never divulged her true identity. A special Careno handout was
prepared and, apart from those close to her, no one knew she
was an opera singer.

Ivor Newton, who met her as Careno later in London was
one of the few in whom she confided, and then only because he

was her accompanist in many classical recitals. He remembers how spectacular she looked on stage, as he says in his book *At the Piano* "like a million dollars". Someone else who retained vivid memories was the musicologist, the late Grenville Eves, who wrote the following extract in an article on her for the journal of the British Institute of Recorded Sound:

> She was always top of the bill. She came on stage wearing a fantastic dress: either of shimmering gold or of pink and silver, sparkling with sequins. Her voice was rich and sensuous and the whole effect was magnificent. Her magnetic personality and striking appearance took hold of the audience in the first minute—an essential quality for success in the Music Hall, where the effect must be immediate if the audience is to be conquered.

After a while a new flavour crept into Careno's publicity, as she and Rabinoff worked out that there was more mileage to be made from her nationality, and even her escape from the Bolsheviks. By now she had convinced most people, even herself at times, that her life had actually been in danger in Russia, so she became a Russian princess who dared not reveal her true identity for fear of reprisals. The *Atlanta Constitution* of Georgia was one of the first papers to cover the story:

> For reasons of her own Madame Careno is playing under a *nom de chantée*. She is really a Russian princess and is beginning to grow restive under her disguise. Her own name is established in the Court circles of Petrograd and Paris. Her assumed one is enshrined in the esteem of American vaudeville patrons.
>
> She is weary of leading a double life. She entered vaudeville thinking she could earn a few weeks pay (she was forced to leave her wealth and jewels behind in Russia). Then audiences made her famous overnight.

Then the *Manitoba Free Press* inquired: "Is this Ganna Walska newspapers often ask but her glorious voice tells them they are mistaken. Others place her as a member of a Russian Grand Duke's family."

Rather late in the day the *Seattle Sunday News* panted out: ". . . it can now be told to a palpitating public that Madame Careno is none other than a Russian princess. She had to hide her identity from the war lords whilst making her way to America."

The princess's coast-to-coast tour lasted six months and no sooner was it over than she was booked to do another. In addition there were many cabaret appearances. Careno's fame spread abroad and there were offers of appearances from London and the continent.

Of course none of this made her happy. Accepting that being a star agreed with her, no sooner had she become used to Variety than she missed her recitals. She felt she was demeaning herself and should be doing better things. She never shook off the feeling that she was lowering her standards, even though "Vissi d'arte", "Un bel di", "Pleurez, mes yeux", "Divinités du Styx" and "O malheureuse Iphigénie" were all part of her act—apart from "Vissi d'arte" and "Un bel di" the rest are all falcon or mezzo arias so there would not be too much strain on her fragile top register—and she almost made a pop song out of Mussorgsky's "Gopak" to which she danced as well as sang. Now and then she would include Gounod's "Ave Maria", during which a stained-glass window would be wheeled on stage, in front of which she would kneel in an attitude of prayer. But this was not highly favoured as there was always the question of getting rid of it for her finale, and it was difficult carting a stained-glass window on wheels about when touring.

She softened her reservations about the inclusion of ballads and popular songs in the act, but those she sang were of quality, requiring a big, strong voice to come across properly.

Her entrance was usually to an elaborate arrangement of Guy d'Hardelot's "Because", during which she swept across the stage in her imperious manner, the train of her gown wafting behind. "Trees" and "For You Alone" were also regulars.

Although Careno made more money than Slobodskaya she began to hate herself as a vaudeville queen. In Oda's old age Careno was a forbidden topic and few knew that she had existed. She was a spectral figure locked in the recesses of Slobodskaya's memory and denied liberty. She was frightened that Careno's flamboyant shadow might tarnish her operatic glory.

Throughout Careno's reign Oda still tried to get work as Slobodskaya and, if it was a question of choice, would invariably accept a recital booking in preference to Variety, even though the fee was far less. Unfortunately there were only a dribble of classical bookings for her and she could only accept some of these as, due to Careno's contractual bookings, her only free day was a Sunday.

There were, however, a few highlights and one of these was a concert with the Boston Symphony Orchestra under the great Pierre Monteux, where she sang arias from *Pique Dame* and *Prince Igor*.

It was overwhelming for her to sing again with a symphony orchestra after the theatre bands, with whom she constantly feuded and insisted were the bane of her life. As another of her accompanists, Ralph Johns, says, "She gave them hell."

The choreographer Fokine had staged a ballet based on the music of Ippolitoff-Ivanov and needed a soloist "to give oriental colour to the thing". Although Fokine wanted the voice to appear disembodied, which meant that Oda had to sing from the wings, she was so delighted to be back in her familiar environment of classical artists that she enjoyed the whole thing.

Her following engagement brought her back to earth and Careno back into harness. It was to sing "Song of India" at a fashion show while the mannequins paraded the latest ladies' clothes.

She was cheered by a letter from her sister Eva who had also managed to escape from Russia and was coming to America to join her. With Oda's help she managed to get a job as a schoolteacher, apparently she had been doing the same sort of thing in Russia. Oda said that Eva made a success of America but if this is so then the following anecdote, which she would tell in a sepulchral voice, is suspect: "Eva had to reprimand a naughty child and locked him in a cupboard as a punishment, and she went home and forgot him. Next morning he was dead. It was terrible." She relished this story, it was one of her favourites. As bookings for Careno continued to pour in from abroad, she accepted an engagement to star for two weeks at London's Palladium theatre. She had spent nearly seven years in America and, by now, the American way of life had become part of her make-up, particularly in her attitude to agents and impresarios.

3*

Work was plentiful and she became careless about ringing people back and keeping appointments. They could wait, if she did not want to do a thing then she did not do it. Which is an unwise policy. Agents have long memories.

CHAPTER SEVEN

ODA SAW FIT to drop the princess image for England, largely because an artist called Princess Yurievska, who claimed kinship with the Tsar, was herself topping bills around the country with a singing act. Although not startling, the princess had a voice which listeners have described as charming; her theatrical costume seemed a touch incongruous in that she favoured a Red Cross uniform, with the addition of a veil. Presumably so that the Bolsheviks would not recognize her.

Wisely Oda decided to revert to the truth, or a semblance of it anyway. In the spring of 1930 *The Star* carried the following item:

Odali Careno is famous all over the continent and throughout the United States and South America.

In London until two or three weeks ago, she was not so well known. Then she appeared and took the place by storm. Seldom have I heard a singer in a music-hall receive so many encores.

This week she is paying a return visit and she has also been booked for further appearances in London.

Miss Careno has had a remarkable career of hardship, triumph and adventure. The qualities of her fine soprano voice were early recognized and while studying music in Italy and Russia she set herself the task of acquiring languages.

Today she sings and talks fluently in twelve tongues: "I was the star dramatic soprano of the Imperial Opera in Petrograd," she told me, "when the revolution broke out. The Bolsheviks decided they required my services so I continued to sing.

"But then, instead of singing for a large salary I was, quite literally, singing for my supper, and not a very good supper at that. It is true that during one month my pay amounted to 60,000 roubles, but when this dazzling total had been translated into terms of bodily sustenance, this is what I got:

1 lb. butter; a little oil; one dozen eggs; 5 lb. bread; 5 lb. potatoes.

"But for the fact that I had concert engagements between times, I and my family would have starved.

"All my jewels, furs and other items of prosperity were exchanged for food, and ultimately we artists dropped altogether the farce of accepting payment in cash. We gave concerts for which the price of admission was food.

"For instance, one pound of butter purchased a very good balcony seat, and a roast of meat secured a whole box."

Oda adored London, particularly the taxi drivers, whom she found so courteous after their American counterparts. She liked the ways of the English and the slower pace of life. She appreciated the aristocracy and approved of the British tradition that one might be impoverished but still have style.

The Londoners seemed to reciprocate her love. As *The Stage* reporter noted, "A third return to the Palladium within eight weeks is a tremendous compliment to any artist, but this has been fully deserved by Odali Careno who, whenever she appears, is a decided 'hit'. Her voice is perfect."

Oda so enjoyed London that she decided not to return to America, despite Rabinoff's pleas about previous bookings. She let him sort that out.

But she was wary of Careno, who seemed all set to parallel her American career in Britain, and decided that Slobodskaya must be reinstated.

Before doing so, though, she had to fulfil a prestigious Careno engagement, a Royal Variety Performance to be held at the Palladium in the presence of Their Majesties King George V and Queen Mary. The dignity of the occasion threw Oda a little: "It was a good job I was wearing a long dress, otherwise Their Majesties might have seen my knees knocking together."

Apparently Queen Mary was greatly taken by Oda's gown, and Oda swore that Her Majesty ordered her couturier to make a replica; presumably Oda had not worn the one with a slit to mid thigh for that occasion.

Oda was convinced she would find artistic satisfaction in London and although Careno was earning up to £500 a week she was determined to kill her off.

She took lodgings at the Langham Hotel, next to Broad-casting House, and her bedroom gave her a view of the Queen's Hall where she was to give many recitals.

Her vocal equipment was given an overhaul by Madame Carlotte de Feo, a distinguished singing teacher resident in London with whom she started to study. Madame de Feo could rectify any sloppiness or faults in her delivery which might have crept in during her Variety act.

1931 saw her putting this coaching to good use as she took part in Dargomijsky's opera *Russalka*, at the Lyceum Theatre. This was really a vehicle for Chaliapine but she was the obvious choice of soprano, having worked successfully with him in Russia. At the time of casting Chaliapine was in Paris, so Oda crossed the Channel to see him.

The meeting was a success and the two singers fell on each other's shoulders and wept profusely, in the manner of Russians who have not seen each other for many years. They reminisced about their friends in Russia and dwelt in depth on those who had perished. Slobodskaya sang an aria from *Russalka* for Chaliapine and he entertained his guests by mimicking some of the singers with whom he had appeared.

Back in London, and on stage at the Lyceum, they worked well together and Ivor Newton recalls, again in *At the Piano*, an occasion when Chaliapine focused all the attention on Oda by standing rock still throughout her aria and concentrating on her.

This was the first time Oda had sung in opera since *Mavra*, nine years before, so a certain coyness is understandable when she writes:

Chaliapine made the part of the miller very much his own. But, as a young singer, just starting out, I think I deserve some merit in sharing a performance with such a great figure. But I lived up to it and it gave me great prestige. I was put on the map straight away.

The "young singer, just starting out" had already succeeded in two distinct careers, in separate continents, and was now about to embark on another in Britain. But perhaps she meant she was new to British audiences. The self-praise in her comments on *Russalka* is because she was chagrined all her life by people who identified her as the lady who had sung with Chaliapine. She wanted recognition as herself, not as someone's co-singer.

Slobodskaya had a chronic problem with her nationality. Throughout her American sojourn she had had to carry work permits and legal documents and had not been granted an American passport. The same problem applied in Britain and she had to visit Paris between engagements to satisfy some technicality about work permits.

It was a frustrating situation which was happily resolved when the unexpected happened and she fell in love.

CHAPTER EIGHT

ODA HAD HAD previous affairs but had kept her feelings under control and the affairs strictly secret so as not to interfere with her career. But now it was the real thing.

The object of her passion was Captain Raymond Henry Arthur Pelly, an army officer of independent means from a good family. He sported a toothbrush moustache and, when not in uniform, plus-fours. He was the epitome of chivalry.

Raymond Pelly came to Careno's dressing-room to compliment her after a performance. Mischa de la Motte, who was billed as the BBC's Five Voice Entertainer, was on the bill with Oda and talking to her in her dressing-room at the time, and remembers the occasion. Mr de la Motte was himself an ardent admirer of Careno and he had already declared his adoration of her in his own, individual style. It had happened when Careno had come off stage and was still in her flame dress. Mr de la Motte knelt and kissed the toe of one of her tomato-coloured shoes:

"I love you," he said.

"Ah, Mischa, but whom do you love? Is it Odali the woman, or Careno the prima donna?"

"Both."

This reply was well received and the diva conceded a chaste kiss on the cheek.

With the captain, however, she was far more roused and he, in turn, was dazzled by her. Being a man of the world he invited her to dine with him at Scott's Restaurant, and she accepted. But her memory of that evening seems to be centred on the menu rather than romance: "He was pleased with the knowledgeable way I ordered things, as women do not usually know much about food. I had a good dish of oysters, which I can't resist, grilled sturgeon and a thick steak."

Their courtship was brief and intense and in no time they were engaged. They married on 28 June 1932, at Bangor Register

Office. and on the marriage certificate Oda puts her age as 37. She was in fact 42, but had already adopted her life-long habit of docking her age. Marriage automatically granted her British citizenship and this put an end to the tedious business of being stateless.

She sang for her new in-laws and her mother-in-law likened her to Melba. This was obviously meant as a compliment but demonstrates that Mrs Pelly had a limited knowledge of singing as the two voices are totally dissimilar. Melba was high coloratura with a unique timbre which has been compared to a choirboy's, and Slobodskaya's voice was low and clarion and ideal for the great heroic rôles. Mrs Pelly did not bother to learn more about music to please her new daughter-in-law as, according to those that knew her, she grew rapidly to dislike her. It is not known what Oda did to displease her but the two women did not hit it off. Possibly they both loved Raymond Pelly.

In the normal course of events Oda would not have lost sleep over anyone's dislike of her but on this occasion it was rather more serious. Not because Mrs Pelly was her mother-in-law but because Mrs Pelly was the source of Raymond's well-being. To put it candidly Mr Pelly, Snr, being deceased, she held the purse strings.

After a short honeymoon the newly weds moved into the house in Iver, Buckinghamshire, in which they were to start their married life. This belonged to Mrs Pelly as did most of the furnishings. Oda did her best to be interested in the house-keeping and, fortunately, the captain was a keen chef. As Oda gaily puts it:

> Raymond did all the cooking and I did the buying. The books we had on cooking would have kept a restaurant going. Some-times he taught me how to cook simple dishes and I would serve them to him with a flourish, and sometimes I made afternoon tea which I served in the garden.
>
> Our house had a lovely garden with an oak tree in the centre and a bed of roses at the bottom. How I loved that cosy home of mine. We were happy there and it was ideal, as I realized every moment we spent together.

Taking tea in the garden was all very pleasant but she couldn't play the lady of leisure for ever. Captain Pelly would have been delighted had she elected to do so, as would her mother-in-law, but the stage was in Oda's blood and she was restless to be performing again.

By now, thanks to Madame de Feo, with whom she still constantly studied, her voice was in excellent condition. She was ready for an assault on the concert platform. With Raymond beside her it was no longer so pressing for her to earn money as Careno, she could concentrate on serious music.

Nevertheless, she still had to honour Careno's commitments, and one of these was at the Winter Garden, Bournemouth. The eminent Sir Dan Godfrey was the conductor and Mischa de la Motte was again on the bill with her. He recalls:

When Sir Dan first heard her sing he nearly fell off his rehearsal stool with surprise. He'd been expecting a standard Variety artist but realized he'd got far more than that.

After rehearsals he knocked on her dressing-room door and asked her surely she had sung in opera? Oda revealed that she was, in fact, Slobodskaya and Sir Dan was intrigued.

He rearranged the programme so that she would have two spots and included in the second half Beethoven's "Ah! perfido" which he substituted for "For You Alone" which she had intended to sing.

Madame de Feo was in the audience at Bournemouth and delighted about Oda's performance. She wrote to her friend, Sir Hamilton Harty, in Manchester, and asked him to hear Oda and use his influence to have her included in the Promenade concerts. Sir Hamilton must have held Madame de Feo's judgement in esteem, for he replied that her recommendation was enough and if Oda could learn, in English, Sieglinde's part from the first act of *Die Walküre*, she could go straight into a Promenade rehearsal.

This was precisely what Oda was working towards and she was ecstatic. She immediately arranged to study with the great expert Charles Webber so that her part would be immaculate and no one could say she was less than perfect.

Oda loved rehearsing and would spend hours going through her music, but Captain Pelly was not so enthusiastic; as Oda put it: "Unfortunately he couldn't stand Wagner, and my first entrée on the British concert platform was Wagner. So I ensured I was nowhere near him when I rehearsed. It would have driven him mad."

She took a room at the Wigmore Hall Rehearsal Studios and learnt her music there.

She was soon to learn that it was not just Wagner to which her husband objected. Neither did he take to the ways of the theatrical crowd which surrounded her. He instructed one artist, who threw his arms about Oda in greeting, "Take your hands off my wife, sir."

Oda's Promenade concert heralded the start of a whole series of regular appearances at the Proms both at the Queen's Hall and the Royal Albert Hall.

In that same year, 1932, she made her Covent Garden début, singing Fevronia in a concert version of Rimsky-Korsakov's *The Invisible City of Kitezh*. She was back a few months later to sing Venus in Wagner's *Tannhäuser*, this time in a full production and at the express invitation of no less a luminary than Sir Thomas Beecham.

Although Sir Thomas was notorious for his dislike of singers, he seemed to have a soft spot for her. She always considered him the perfect gentleman and said "our relationship was perfectly harmonious". Sir Thomas's *Tannhäuser* had a brilliant cast, including Lotte Lehmann, Lauritz Melchior, Herbert Janssen and Ludwig Hoffman.

By engaging Slobodskaya, Sir Thomas was, unwittingly, instrumental in repairing a tiff that had blown up between her and the captain. They had exchanged sharp words and, in a fit of pique, Oda had sailed to Paris, leaving no forwarding address except with her agents, Ibbs and Tillet, and they were instructed not to divulge this to anyone, specifically the captain, who did not even know that she had left the country.

Sir Thomas was no anyone, he was someone, and, thanks to Ibbs and Tillett, he had no difficulty in locating the errant wife in Paris and telephoning her. Was she familiar with the part of Venus, he asked? Of course, she replied, although she had never set eyes on the score. Would she be available to sing this at Covent Garden on 23 May? She certainly would. She was engaged over the telephone and told rehearsals started within a few days.

Putting all thoughts of the quarrel behind her, Oda caught the first available boat to England and bought a copy of the *Tannhäuser* score before reaching home.

It was hard work learning the part in time. Venus is a demanding rôle and with Lotte Lehmann in the cast Oda had strong competition. She could not afford to be unsure of herself. Even the captain put his dislike of Wagner aside and rallied round:

> Although Wagner was not pleasing to my husband he assisted me at rehearsals. I can only say this was a wonderful period in my life. Engaged at Covent Garden, being in love, and good food, who could ask for more? We were blissfully happy. The only thing that could have been better was my husband's health, he was frail.

In order to give his wife a break from studying, the captain took Oda to the country for a day of wine-tasting. He was a connoisseur but Oda knew nothing about wines and cared less. Although devoted to good food she rarely took even a glass of wine and never touched spirits. This did not stop her from enjoying herself at the wine festival though, and she sportingly tasted all the varying wines and, probably as a release from the stress she had been undergoing, got rolling and happily drunk for the first and only time in her life. She was laughing and calling out of the window as her homeward-bound train left the platform. The captain was not amused.

Oda's most enduring memory of Venus was of one rehearsal when an oboist arrived late and Sir Thomas was, for once, on time. When the man saw the maestro and the full orchestra waiting for him he ran down the aisle in a panic. Not being a youngster he puffed as he took his place:

"Give me an A," commanded Sir Thomas.

The oboe player put his instrument to his lips and blew. Naturally the note wavered a little.

"Gentlemen," said Sir Thomas to the orchestra. "Take your pick."

Beecham so liked Oda that he invited her to make a film with him, a biography of Mozart with which he was involved. Oda did not appear but her voice was used on the soundtrack. It is odd that Beecham should have chosen her as she was certainly not a Mozartian singer. But she was probably very good, it is a great pity the film seems to have disappeared.

After Venus she sailed to Buenos Aires for a season of Russian opera at the Teatro Colon. She sang in three works, Fevronia in *Kitezh*; Marina in *Boris Godunov* and Militrissa in Rimsky-Korsakov's *Tsar Sultan*.

In 1933 she was at La Scala to sing in a season of Russian opera produced under the direction of Emile Cooper. She sang the same three works but this time in Italian.

After a brief return to Britain she sailed to Holland to sing the soprano part in Beethoven's Ninth symphony, under Mengelberg. He was impressed by the unusual timbre of her voice and suggested that Richard Strauss' Salome might suit her. The work had not been performed in Britain since 1906 but Oda bought a copy of the score and learned the title part. Her agents contacted the BBC, and the Corporation agreed to broadcast the work under the direction of Albert Coates. Perhaps she was prejudiced but Oda considered *Salome* was better performed on radio than on stage: "I prefer it not to be seen. It is so revolting when John's head is brought in on a platter. Quite disgusting."

Salome started a lasting and profitable relationship with the BBC, and she became a regular contributor to the Third Programme. Quite a few important Russian works had their British radio première through Slobodskaya: she introduced Prokofiev's *The Love of Three Oranges*; Tchaikovsky's *Pique Dame* (the opera in which she had made her Marynsky début) and Shostakovitch's *Lady Macbeth of Mtsinsk*, later retitled *Katerina Ismailova*.

The latter was quite an event as, at that time, the Iron Curtain was securely pulled down and little contemporary music left Russia. But part of the score was smuggled into Britain and Slobodskaya was the obvious choice to sing these excerpts. They were performed at a concert organized by The Society for Modern Music, at the Aeolian Hall in Bond Street. Among the items was the big, main aria and this was broadcast live by the BBC:

I found Shostakovitch more rewarding to sing than Stravinsky and not so overpowering as Richard Strauss. Rhythmically it is simple, although one has to watch out for difficult intervals.

I sang to a packed house, never before or since have I sung

to such a packed hall, they were standing along the walls, it was very thrilling.

Later she broadcast the entire work but the critics were unenthusiastic about the piece.

At the time these cultural activities were taking place she did a quick revert to Careno. She was at the BBC to discuss a forthcoming broadcast and ran into a Light Entertainment producer who knew her as Careno, and persuaded her to take part in a *Workers' Playtime* programme the following day. She did not want to turn down the fee so agreed and gave a quick blast of "For You Alone" and "Because" in a works canteen. No harm was done. Radio work may seem insignificant today but in those pre-television and pre-LP days radio was the only source of music for many people, and regular broadcasts assured fame.

It is impossible to list the numerous concerts and recitals Slobodskaya gave in the 1930s. She took part in a Promenade concert each year where, in addition to her regular repertoire, she sang Mendelssohn's "Infelice", the closing scene from *Salome* and Cassandra's aria from Berlioz's *Les Troyens*, the latter ideally suiting her voice.

By now, probably partly due to the strain of the high tessitura of *Salome*, she was beginning to lose some of her highest notes, the tones that Iretskaya artificially created for her, and the voice, while still majestic, settled down to its true register, that of mezzo, although still retaining soprano colour. Gone forever were the lovely, floating, high pianissimos. She could still produce a high C but not as she did at the Marynsky: "I did a broadcast of 'Ocean, Thou Mighty Monster' and when I got home my husband said to me, 'My dear, that top C was dreadful.' He was right, it was. That C is optional and I never used it again."

Now and then her slightly failing powers unnerved her. At an Albert Hall concert she was to sing an aria from *Die Walküre*. She was suddenly frightened that it was too high for her and, white and trembling, turned to Carlotte de Feo, who was with her in the wings, and told her she dare not go on. The shock nearly caused Madame de Feo to faint and she had to be given brandy and sat down. So she was not really a great help. Slobodskaya was convinced the evening would be a disaster and paced about groaning and holding her head. Various artists and production people tried to restore her confidence; it must have been chaos.

When her opening music came Slobodskaya walked on to the platform in terror, but disaster was averted: "Carlotte told me that as soon as she heard my voice ring out she knew I would be all right, and she could breathe again."

Of course she was all right.

Not so satisfactorily executed though was another Albert Hall concert. This time it was not her voice that caused concern but her wardrobe.

The concert was in mid-winter and Oda arrived at the Albert Hall clad for the weather in Wellington boots. She brought a friend to help her dress. The friend had never been backstage before and was intrigued by it all, and wandered away leaving Slobodskaya to dress herself, which she did, with rather ill humour. She was to sing the Letter Scene from *Eugene Onegin* and it was being simultaneously broadcast.

When her cue came she walked out to the auditorium and bowed to the audience—and found herself staring at her Wellington boots which peeped from beneath her long frock. Forgetting she was being broadcast live she marched straight off the platform and back to her dressing-room in a fury. The friend saw her coming and ran away, out of the hall, which was sensible. God knows how the BBC commentator explained the awful silence after Madame Slobodskaya had been introduced. Another singer might have stood there in Wellington boots but not Slobodskaya. She loved her elegant clothes and would not countenance appearing without her sparkling shoes.

An even more embarrassing incident happened at the studios in Broadcasting House, where she was to broadcast a live recital.

Arriving just before her accompanist, she was just a little agitated as she was having trouble with her stocking suspenders. Finding herself alone in the studio she hoisted up her skirt and adjusted the troublesome undergarment. In mid-action her glance rested on a glass partition which started half-way up the wall and continued to the ceiling. This was soundproofed and behind it sat an audience assembled to hear the recital which would be fed to them via speakers. They were eagerly watching her.

Both these stories were favourites of Oda's, although she only related the latter to intimate friends.

In 1935 she was again singing at Covent Garden under Beecham, this time in the seldom heard Delius opera *Koanga*. When engaging Oda, Sir Thomas was charm itself and indulged in a genteel little leg-pull. Oda would tell how he summoned her to his office:

Knowing of his fondness for the ladies I made sure I looked my best with a smart business suit and a gorgeous new blouse.

I said to him, "I understand, Sir Thomas, you would like me to sing the part of Palmeera?"

He did not answer for a while and I was so young and inexperienced I did not know what to do. He stroked his beard and eventually said, "We say Palmyra here, but I think I like your Palmeera better."

He was so charming we never had the slightest misunderstanding. He may have had a reputation for rudeness but never with me.

During rehearsals Oda was amused by Tommy Chapman, the rehearsal pianist, who persistently fell asleep. Sir Thomas had to shout to wake him up. Tommy would jump as though he had been shot but come in at once with exactly the right chord.

Oda wore an exotic headdress for *Koanga* and, Ivor Newton recalls, Beecham never forgot this: "It seemed to go on for ever," he said. "Up and up and up." She wrote in her diary about *Koanga*:

Dear Sir Thomas rehearsed with a great deal of care and tried to correct things he felt Delius had not fulfilled.

Despite his efforts *Koanga* was not popular and it has again been put on the shelf. Not for too long, I hope.

She caused quite a stir at the Proms that year during her singing of an aria from *Jeanne d'Arc*:

I was so moved by the despair at the end of the piece that I laid my head on the shoulder of the first violinist as I sang.

This stands out in my memory as one of the best things I

ever did for the audience went wild with excitement. I can
dwell on this outstanding performance with pleasure, things
don't always work out that well.

Afterwards the conductor came to my room and told me,
"Madame, I have heard that aria a number of times, but never
like that."

Another happy memory is "Chanson Perpetuelle". I was
singing this at the BBC and Moura Lympany was listening.
When I finished she said, "Oda, when you sing it always *means*
so much." She meant my interpretation.

In 1937 she notched up another success but this time tinged
with sadness:

I went to Palestine to sing with Issay Dobrowen and the
Palestine Orchestra. I sang some Mossoloff songs and "Ah!
perfido".

The concert was a great success. Paul Muni, the actor, was
there and as I left the hall after my performance, he handed me
his scarf saying, "Put this round your neck, you must protect
that golden voice of yours." Although I had been given more
expensive presents before, his simple consideration touched
me deeply.

I'm sorry to say that I went to Palestine without my husband,
and I'll never forgive myself for this. He did not want me to
go without him but the company refused to pay two fares and
I did not have the courage to insist. I had no pleasure from
that trip as my heart was longing for home all the time. Ray
would have loved to have seen the ancient city of Jerusalem.

I should have gone to the places of interest in Palestine, but
my restless heart would give me no peace until I saw my
husband again. I made my way home as soon as I finished the
concert. Life is full of remorse and this is mine.

CHAPTER NINE

IN 1939 WAR broke out and London was a dismal place. Due to the blitz, houses and shops disappeared overnight. Any food shop that had stock had queues outside, and the queuers jealously guarded their ration books. At night the city was blacked-out. All lights were extinguished so as to give no geographical indication to the enemy bombers. Every window had thick, black curtains and should the slightest chink of light show the police would knock at the door. There were no street lights and traffic was at a minimum. Men were away fighting and women were alone and frightened, not knowing if their husbands and boyfriends were alive, dead or prisoners.

This was the London in which Oda now found herself. It was a time of tragedy for everyone and she was just another victim of the war:

> My peaceful life came to an end. The bombing did not worry me particularly but Ray was terrified.
>
> As the German assault intensified he became ill with nerves and his heart began to suffer. I did everything I could to help him and make him feel at ease. But the strain was too much and his health gave way. His illness grew worse and he died. I lost him.

She was heartbroken. They had had many quarrels and she had left him once, but they were fond of each other and now she was totally alone. For with Ray's death contact with the Pelly family ceased.

Oda kept a bundle of letters that the captain had written her from time to time and these were tied together with a green ribbon. Time and again she would take this little bundle from the drawer in which it was kept, kiss it and cry. Eventually the envelopes became smudged with the lipstick and this formed red pools where it had run with the water from her tears.

As she could not bear to live in Iver without Ray she moved back into town and shared a flat with a woman friend.

The bombing raids did not frighten her. She was so unhappy she would have welcomed a direct hit. Cruellest of all, now that she desperately needed work to take her mind off Ray, there was nothing. People were frightened to go to theatres in case they were bombed and Russians were unpopular due to Russia's war strategy. There was nothing for her to do but sit in her shared flat and mourn:

There was no work for me and no concerts. The Queen's Hall was bombed and everything was at a standstill.

I was disliked for being Russian and people were rude to me. But was it my fault where I was born? Did I have anything to do with the war? I do not understand politics, all I wanted to do was sing.

A glimmer of hope shone through the dullness and she clutched at it:

Val Drury rang me and asked if I would be prepared to do some work for the war organizations, CEMA and ENSA, and to sing in shelters, hospitals and camps and entertain the troops in general. My fee would be 30/- [£1.50p] a concert, plus transport and tea. I was more than grateful.

I plunged into the work immediately, and did lots of travelling and singing. All for duty and none for pleasure. Anyway, I had to do something to keep sane. My aching heart was like a dead weight, and pain and grief never left me for a second. I sang everywhere, even in underground stations, sometimes singing under falling splinters. It was difficult to find the right address at night as all lights were forbidden and the streets in darkness. I was usually alone but, somehow, I made my way and when I got there I was in danger of being killed at any moment. But who cared? I had lost my husband and was indifferent to what might happen.

The work was a relief and I took it seriously. If there was no proper hall then I sang for the people in the middle of the street and, more than once, pieces of shrapnel landed within a few feet of me. I didn't stop or even move, I just kept on singing.

I tried to sing as many songs and arias as possible in English, and also included ballads and popular songs, which I think ordinary people preferred.

I once sang in a hospital for mental diseases and my high notes caused a strange reaction in a woman patient, who couldn't take them and collapsed, unconscious, falling under the piano. Two attendants came and took her away but I continued with my aria the whole time.

Another time I was singing for the blind and the guide dogs started howling but I still carried on.

Often the warning system sounded, indicating bombers overhead, but I did not interrupt my song. This must be a trait in my nature—whatever happened, bells ringing, bombs falling, shrapnel flying or patients collapsing, I carried on regardless.

Although recitals did not exist for Slobodskaya at that time, the BBC regularly used her and, as she said "they kept me from starvation". Apart from her widow's pension she received nothing but her earnings.

People might be frightened to go out at night but they gladly attended concerts in their lunch hours. So Dame Myra Hess founded a scheme for mid-day recitals at the National Gallery. But for her, many artists might not have been seen at all during the war. Slobodskaya was delighted to sing at the National Gallery and, whatever the climate of political opinion, stuck to her repertoire:

I sang all my Russian songs there, and so my work continued. That beloved man, Edwin Evans, prepared all my programme translations and they sold for a penny each. I treasure all those penny programmes, they are so dear to me. For the lunch-time concerts we received five guineas and were lucky to get it.

As no one seemed to have much opportunity to hear anyone else perform, a group of Russian musicians fell into the habit of meeting to commiserate at the home of pianist Vera Bennison,

herself a Russian who had married an Englishman. The conductor
Anatole Fistoulari and Oda were among those who used to
visit:

> Life was flat and these meetings cheered us up, and sometimes
> good ideas came to light. Fistoulari was full of plans to bring
> neglected Russian music to the public, and one evening told
> us he intended to produce and conduct Mussorgsky's
> *Sorochinsky Fair*. He had met a wealthy enthusiast who agreed
> to finance it. If we all agreed the opera could be staged at the
> Savoy Theatre and rehearsals start the following week.

That last sentence is a masterpiece of omission. There were
heated feelings over the casting of *Sorochinsky Fair* and
temperaments flared.

Slobodskaya assumed she would be offered the soprano part of
Parassia, and indeed, she had made a gramophone record of
Parassia's aria for HMV in 1931 (see Recordings, part three),
but Parassia was already cast to a young newcomer called Daria
Bayan. All that remained to offer Oda was the secondary mezzo
rôle of Khivria, the part written for comic relief.

A pretty little scene ensued at Mrs Bennison's when the truth
eventually filtered through to her. But, as Maestro Fistoulari has
pointed out: "It was ridiculous for her to sing Parassia, quite
simply she was too old. Parassia is a young girl and Oda was in
her 50s."

So it was a case of accepting Khivria or doing without a part.
Her diary records the entry, with some restraint:

> There was a little anxiety in case I should refuse. Khivria's
> part is mezzo and I had always sung soprano. But I accepted,
> and reasoned that a mezzo part is a test of ability. Added to
> this, Khivria has the very best of Mussorgsky's music. He
> didn't finish the opera and the first and last acts contain many
> revisions and additions by Tcherepnin.

She appeared mostly in the second act. Yet, she grew to like
the part and showed a hitherto unknown flair for comedy: "It
was full of gorgeous folk melodies and appealed to my sense of
humour. The music inspired me to learn all Mussorgsky's songs.

As for the money, well, that was the least consideration. Among Russians money is considered of little importance."

She had her own ethics concerning money. If she particularly wanted a part then the fee was secondary; for example, she received little for *Koanga*, as was discovered purely by chance by her future Decca record producer, Christopher Raeburn. In a curio shop he came across the endorsed cheque with which Beecham had paid her. Thinking she would be touched he had it mounted and sent it to her as a gift. But it was never displayed. She told him, "I thank you for your cheque but I dare not put it out. I do not want anyone to see how little I received."

On the other hand, Ralph Johns, who accompanied her in her Careno days remembers an instance when she asked him to play for her in Blackpool, where she was topping the bill and getting over £500 a week. He insisted she pay his fare from London to Blackpool, by which suggestion she was outraged. Eventually, when it became clear that if she did not she might well be singing unaccompanied she relented and agreed to give him an additional £5 out of her own pocket, her agents would settle his fees. When the time came for Johns to collect the £5 she took a thick wad of notes from her handbag, peeled one off, and told him "Now you are rich", making it clear this was at her expense.

There's an interesting rider to this. Ralph was so tired by his long journey from London to Blackpool (these were pre-Inter-city days and he was performing the same day as he travelled) that when they were on stage and Careno was announcing to the audience what she would next sing, Ralph, sitting at the piano, rested his head in his hands and, unfortunately, fell asleep. When she waited for the introduction to her song there was silence. It was obvious to both artist and audience what had happened, and the audience roared. Oda laughed gaily too, as she woke Ralph by playfully jabbing her fingers in his neck.

But in her frame of mind previous to *Sorochinsky Fair* she would gladly have played Khivria for nothing.

Rehearsals, which were at the Wigmore Hall, did not go too smoothly. The backer was a Mr Jay Pomeroy, who was Russian despite his English-sounding surname, and who was known as Pommy to the cast. As he was providing the money for the venture, he decided he had the right to air his views on the production and, when the occasion demanded, would address the cast from the stage. It is regrettable that what he said was usually at variance with the views of the producer, George Kirsta. Naturally Mr Pomeroy had to back down and Oda felt a little sorry for him: "It was difficult to support Pommy's ideas for, although his heart was in the right place, he did not know a great deal about the theatre, and nothing at all about *Sorochinsky Fair*."

The opera opened at the Savoy Theatre in 1941 and was a great success. It then went on a British tour and returned to the West End, this time at the Adelphi Theatre. As with all productions there was the usual amount of clowning about on stage: "One night I had a great joke with the singer playing the clergyman. At one point he has to crawl inside a chest and then crawl out. But I sat on top so the lid couldn't open and stayed there as long as possible, it was great fun."

It was as well that Oda enjoyed herself in *Sorochinsky Fair* for, had she been able to see into the future, it is doubtful if she could have borne what was in store for her.

CHAPTER TEN

SLOBODSKAYA'S CAREER NEVER recovered from the effects of the war. Years later, when Sylvia Fisher asked her why there had been such a gap in her career, she replied disarmingly, "I don't think they wanted me."

She was aware that her voice must eventually deteriorate and was desperate to make records while still in good form. She wanted to record "Pleurez, mes yeux", "Ah! perfido", "Divinités du Styx" and Jeanne d'Arc's aria in particular. None of these was ever recorded.

To her horror, Slobodskaya found herself joining the ranks of the unemployed, taking her place in the realms of the has-beens. Years dragged by and, whereas it cannot be said nothing happened, there was little of interest except that her voice did, inexorably, deteriorate. With this diminishing of her powers she seemed to lose her zest for life.

She had no home life now, and agents showed little interest in her and she was too dispirited to chase after them. Sometimes she would get out her bundle of letters from Ray, and hold them to her cheek and cry. "From my darlink," she would sob, and seemed to get comfort from their closeness.

In desperation she made an attempt to resurrect the hated Careno, as anything was better than poverty and idleness. It was a pathetic attempt as she was far too old to play the glamorous songstress. The British agents dismissed the idea out of hand.

Not despairing, she decided to try her luck in America again, which was, after all, Careno's birthplace. Fearful, but full of hope, she invested a good slice of her diminishing capital on a plane ticket to New York. But the Americans were even less interested and not even polite about their rejection. She never forgave the Americans that second visit. She sat on the plane on her return flight full of hatred and misery. The famous eau-de-nil dress was still wrapped in its cellophane, it had not even been unpacked.

To add to her depression she learned, when she returned to

London, that Elisabeth Schwarzkopf was preparing some arias from *Eugene Onegin*, and she was indignant that that lady did not come to her for coaching: "she deserves to fail," she said.

The gloom lightened momentarily when an agent approached her with plans for a tour of Australia, but these were dropped within days because of the expense involved.

When the Boulting brothers asked her to appear in an important new film called *The Magic Box* she was ecstatic. Its première was scheduled to coincide with the opening of the Festival of Britain in 1951. The cast included Robert Donat, Richard Attenborough, Robert Beatty, Stanley Holloway, Glynis Johns, Bernard Miles, Laurence Olivier, Joyce Grenfell, Eric Portman, Michael Redgrave and Margaret Rutherford. Her part, as an over-blown prima donna, was small and included no dialogue, but, at the time, it was monumentally important to her.

She was unsure on the set as this was her first appearance in a film, she had only sung on the soundtrack of the Mozart biography. The hectic atmosphere and sheer verve of the studio frightened her, it was so different from stage work. But she found a friend in Joyce Grenfell who took her under her wing and looked after her. As far as Miss Grenfell was concerned Oda was simply "an endearing character and I tried to show her the ropes". To Oda's ultra-sensitive temperament though, this kindness in a hostile atmosphere was a momentous thing. She never forgot Joyce Grenfell's kindness.

A lecture-recital tour of South Africa was arranged for 1953 and this seemed the break for which she had been waiting. She could take to the road again with her head held high. But it was disaster from the outset.

In order to make the trip viable the backers insisted on a fee in the region of £80 per appearance. This is a far from large amount for a concert but she would also be lecturing to schools and colleges which had only limited funds. One official sarcastically ended his letter ". . . of course we know of Madame Slobodskaya's reputation, and should the time arrive when we can afford her services we will notify you. Until that halcyon day we must, reluctantly, content ourselves with less expensive artists."

Finally it was all arranged and the finances agreed. She flew to

Oda Slobodskaya in 1922 during her first vist to Western Europe

Left, Wearing the famous white coat
Right, Odali Careno in New York *c*. 1923

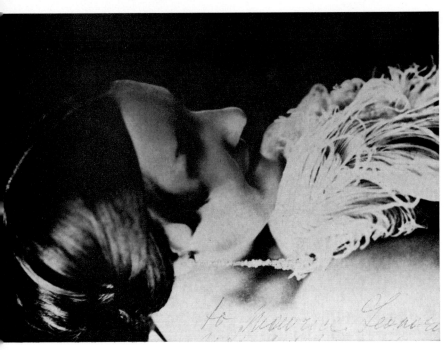

Left, As Odali Careno *c.* 1925
Right, Oda Slobodskaya *c.* 1930

Odali Careno wearing the Chartreuse dress *c.* 1930 (note the single earring)

Slobodskaya in the late thirties, wearing her "Beecham" blouse

Left, Slobodskaya with Alfred Nieman *c.* 1940
Right, At the Royal Albert Hall during the late forties

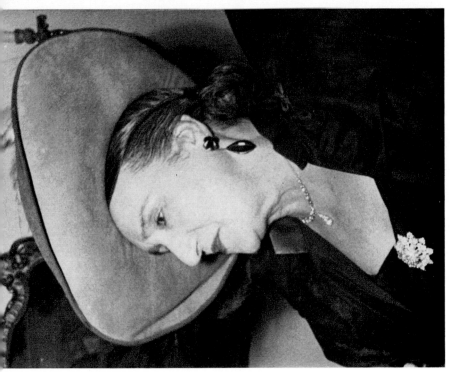

Left, Slobodskaya in 1960
Right, At the St Cecilia Dinner, 1960

Left, Slobodskaya in Donegal with Mr and Mrs Cyril Franklin, in 1968, shortly before she died

Right, In Regent's Park during the early sixties

South Africa confident that, after her weeks of practice, she was singing well.

On arrival someone suggested she see the local sights and took her on a trip to the top of a nearby mountain. Tragically the altitude affected her voice, as can happen with singers, and her entire top register disappeared: "Disaster struck. I couldn't sing for a month and had to cancel all bookings. Everyone went mad, I shan't forget that in a hurry." She came home in tears. It was not her fault but the backers lost a great deal of money and she was the object of considerable ill feeling.

As the 1950s dragged on she sadly reconciled herself to the realization that her career was finished which, in her eyes, meant oblivion. Even the BBC deserted her. Her agents tried to book a radio recital but were told that Oda Slobodskaya was now finished. Incredibly, someone at the agency passed this message on to Oda. Sadly she told her pianist, Annette Holbron, "When the BBC say you are finished, you *are* finished."

Those dreary, grey years seemed to last longer than the rest of her life put together.

Being a practical lady, and incapable of inactivity, she took the only sensible course open to an ageing singer who has a reputation, and decided to teach. It took a little time to persuade the Guildhall School of Music and Drama that they would be fortunate to acquire her services but she eventually succeeded and became a professor of singing. Much later, in 1964, she also joined the staff of the Royal College of Music. In addition she taught privately at the Wigmore Hall studios and at her flat at Ivor Court, where she had moved shortly after her husband's death. For many years her pianist at these lessons was Annette Holbron and she was paid, initially, 2/6d [12½p] an hour which was eventually raised to 5/- [25p] after a great deal of thought and consideration. This is a ludicrously small amount to pay a professional musician but Miss Holbron's reason for accepting the fee is simple: "She had the power to make you love her, even though you knew she was unjust."

Miss Holbron recalls another example of Slobodskaya's injustice coupled with her ability to engender love:

She was waiting for a new pupil to arrive but got restless and wandered off, telling me to wait for the girl.

4

Well, I waited quite a while and then had to answer an urgent call of nature. While I was gone the girl arrived and finding no one in the room left. When Madame Slobodskaya came back she went mad and said it was all my fault she had lost a pupil. I said it wasn't but she would not relent. Eventually I said that if she felt that way it would perhaps be better if we terminated our agreement and she found another pianist. All she said was, "We will see about that." So there was a stony silence for the rest of the afternoon until about teatime. Then, she produced an orange from her bag which she started to peel and, without looking at me, she said slowly, "Would you like a piece of orange?" Everything was all right after that.

Although she had little choice about making a career as a singing teacher, she made the best of it, and always announced publicly that her reason for teaching was that she "wished to pass on her knowledge to a new and younger generation" and she probably meant it.

She took a personal interest in those pupils whom she considered worthy, and this interest was by no means restricted to their musical lives. She had to know everything about the girls, particularly whether or not they had boyfriends. These were frowned upon on principle, although she herself was always receptive to the charms of young men. Annette Holbron remembers one encounter:

She always wore her old clothes when she was teaching and one day, about three of us, including Slobodskaya, popped out from the Guildhall to get a cup of coffee.

When we got back to the Guildhall we realized Slobodskaya had left her muff in the Wimpy Bar, so we had to return. But when we got there it was closed. She hammered on the door until someone came and gave her her muff.

Just as we were about to leave a young man came up and asked if she wasn't Oda Slobodskaya. She went rigid and held the muff taut to her bosom. "Yes," she muttered. He complimented her on some performance he'd seen. Still holding the muff in front of her, and without relaxing at all, she muttered "Thank you," and he went off. "Just think," she said. "It was a man, and he saw me looking like this."

According to many who worked with her, she was not the best of teachers. Certainly she was not always successful with her girls. Christine Bolton, who studied with her for years and helped look after her in her declining years, was trained as a mezzo, she is now singing in her true register, soprano.

Annette Holbron is of the opinion that Slobodskaya's talents were misdirected by the Guildhall School of Music and Drama and the Royal Academy and that, instead of a singing teacher, she should have concentrated on coaching Russian repertoire, in which she was inspired. Her straight-forward voice training was not so remarkable. Like many talented people, her art was effortless and she had little understanding with those who found it difficult. To work well with a professor a pupil must be relaxed. But if Slobodskaya did not take to a girl she could produce the opposite effect in her. One girl was so intimidated by her presence that she could barely speak, let alone sing.

Yet, there were times when she could be caring. Miss Holbron was with her when a young man came for an audition. He was desperately keen to sing tenor rôles and Slobodskaya heard him out. She then gave her opinion that he was a baritone. The poor man had tears in his eyes and raged at her, insisting he was a tenor, he even banged his fist on the table. Miss Holbron expected her to fly into a rage herself at this insolence, instead she also was nearly in tears. "What have I done?" she asked him tenderly. "I am so sorry, believe me, I did not mean to hurt you. I merely tell you what I hear."

Everyone who knew Oda experienced her sharp tongue. Miss Holbron was playing for a pupil whom Oda was coaching in *Trovatore*. As the girl was a soprano Miss Holbron amused herself by filling in the mezzo part, but not for long. She got a sharp dig in the shoulder, "Don't sing, dear, just play the notes."

There are still various professors at the Guildhall who can vouch for her uncertain temperament. She charged at one of these, a man incidentally, like a bull at a matador, when she learned that he'd suggested to a pupil of hers that the girl might be better off under another teacher.

So her life formed a pattern and she settled down to old age. But she wasn't finished yet, and 1959 proved to be one of the most fateful years of her life. She met a remarkable man called Mr W. H. Barrington-Coupe.

CHAPTER ELEVEN

UNTIL 1959 NEARLY all Long Playing records cost in the region of £2, then Saga Records entered the field and caused a revolution, offering quality recordings at 12/6d [62½p].

At first the major companies ignored the upstart. After all, who could compete with the galaxy of talent shared between EMI, Decca, Phillips and RCA? But it soon became apparent that Saga was not going away and that the upstart was making a dent in the profits of the big companies and, therefore, was a force with which to be reckoned.

W. H. Barrington-Coupe was the force behind Saga and his formula for success was to buy deleted matrixes and re-issue these on the Saga label, at less than a third of the original price. Added to this there were original recordings when little-known artists, perhaps graduates, were given a small fee to record.

In the normal course these performers would have been ignored by record producers until they became known. As this could have taken years the artists, naturally, were grateful for the opportunity of making a record under the Saga scheme. Several now-established stars were given a leg up the ladder by Saga and a case in point is Dame Janet Baker. Although this international mezzo had recorded extensively she was comparatively unknown as a soloist to the record-buying public until Saga issued her *Frauenliebe und Leben* in 1966.

At the very outset of his Saga career Mr Barrington-Coupe had the brainwave of approaching Slobodskaya, who had not re-corded for years, and asking her to record for him. He offered her £15 for a dozen or so Russian songs.

Many years previously, when Decca had asked Oda to record, she had vacillated before giving an answer, as she was concerned that Decca did not carry the same prestige as HMV, but now, when Saga, at 12/6d each, offered £15 she snatched at the offer. She was so desperate to record while she still had a shred of voice that she would probably have paid Mr Barrington-Coupe had he asked.

It seemed the answer to her prayers. For years she had harangued the big companies to record her, and her friends had done their best, besieging *The Listener*, *The Gramophone* and other magazines with letters lamenting the lack of Slobodskaya recordings. All to no effect, and just as she had settled down to retirement here was a miracle in the shape of Mr Barrington-Coupe.

Should anyone think that Slobodskaya was duped by receiving only a £15 recording fee, it must be remembered that Saga was a new enterprise with limited capital. Slobodskaya was a has-been and it was possible that the public would be indifferent to the record and not buy. Oda never felt she had been exploited and was always grateful to Mr Barrington-Coupe.

In order to promote the record, Mr Barrington-Coupe arranged a recital for Slobodskaya at the Wigmore Hall. Ivor Newton was to accompany her on the night (as he does, on the record) but, for the many rehearsals, she worked with Annette Holbron who confirms that Oda was tireless and never gave a perfunctory rehearsal.

Slobodskaya's friends were not without misgivings about the concert as she had not given a recital for years. Yet there was no hesitation on her part—this was her last chance and she was reaching for it with both hands.

Her enthusiasm, however, was no protection against hurt and, as she inwardly harboured fears, she was sensitive to callous remarks. More than once quips in the nature of "Is she still alive?" came to her ears, and there was a certain amount of sniggering from that effete section of every operatic and concert audience. The most unforgivable blow came from an official at the Wigmore Hall, a man who certainly should have known better. He was convinced that the concert would be a disaster and that Oda would make a fool of herself. He was not worried about her, it was the waste of time that he resented. Relaying his feelings to Oda, which must have been a blow to her confidence, he stayed away from the performance, and did not even bother to wish her good luck. She never forgave him and, just a few days before her death, was still cursing him.

By the date of the concert she was as fully prepared as she ever would be. Nowadays it took her a little longer to learn new music and certain established items had to be dropped as she no longer had the range to sing them. But the strength of her voice and her dramatic verve had not diminished.

She looked fabulous. Her hair dyed raven and a silver fox slung over her black, velvet dress. Diamanté glittered at her wrists and throat. No one can know what was whirling through her brain as she waited to go on, but it must have been a terrifying moment. Then she took a deep breath and strode out into the lights.

The audience burst into applause, and the hall was packed to such an extent that, for the first time in many years, the balcony had to be opened. It seemed the public had not forgotten her after all. She was shaking with nerves as the applause washed over her, which is not surprising when one considers she was actually 71 years old.

The night of the 30 November 1959 is now musical history but it did not seem that it would be at all memorable at the beginning of the recital. She was too emotional to give of her best and this adversely affected her breath control. There were one or two awkward moments while her voice warmed up, although she was experienced enough to ward off any disasters. Then, about a third of the way through the evening, the prima donna took over and she regained her confidence, and with it her technique. Her vocal mechanism sprang back into place and she was her old self and singing with all the old panache.

And how she sang, song after song, and her voice did not let her down. Perhaps she cracked just once on a Balakirev lullaby but who cared? By now she had won over the audience completely and was only allowed to finally leave the stage after four encores.

Next day it was back to the old routine. She sat up in her bed, pillows propped around her, answering congratulatory calls on the telephone and reading her press. All the papers praised her and now that praise was worth more than gold. No longer could she say "not for me" when someone said a song or aria was difficult. What age had taken from her had to be replaced by effort and artistry. She had reason to be proud.

. . . she retains unimpaired her magnificent powers . . . a large audience last night left no doubt of their appreciation . . . a perfect integration of words and music.   *Daily Telegraph*

. . . connoisseurs of fine singing have tried to take every opportunity of hearing the great Russian soprano Oda Slobodskaya. Her voice today is one of the most beautiful of its kind I've ever heard, strong and rich and thrilling.

. . . Anyone who thought this was to be merely a tribute to the past was soon surprised . . . It is not only her artistry that we admire today, but that impeccable, smooth voice production, the tone and its expressive range, and perhaps above all—since the art seems almost lost—the glorious legato.

She is an unabashed dramatic interpreter. The "Nursery Suite" was mimed as well as sung. . . . To hang with the principle of the thing! Slobodskaya's realism is so vivid that we believe this is the only way to do it. . . . She wheedled and sulked and scolded with complete conviction . . . she brought sensuous beauty, high spirits, or that yearning, sweetly intense sorrow which seems to us so characteristically Russian. . . .

Andrew Porter, *Financial Times*

She showed herself in splendid voice and roused the audience to a pitch of enthusiasm rarely witnessed in our sedate recital rooms.

Desmond Shawe-Taylor, *Sunday Times*

And there were lots more. One of the first people to congratulate her was soprano Dame Isobel Baillie, who telephoned her from her home in Manchester. But even in her hour of glory Oda had her feet on the ground. Dame Isobel recalled that Oda answered, "Yes, it's wonderful. But it's too late, darling."

Another of her congratulators was veteran Carrie Tubb. Apart from her own distinguished career Miss Tubb had another claim to fame in that she was the sister of Dame Clara Butt. Miss Tubb considered Oda ". . . surely one of the most elegant of singers. Her phrasing was always so immaculately tailored, there was never anything crude."

Shortly after the recital and on the crest of her success, Saga released her LP record and this received similar acclamation to the recital. Although she accepted this gratefully, privately Oda did not agree with the critics. She did not like the record and when she heard it burst into tears of anguish. In her mind she still recalled her fresh, young voice and what she heard was an old woman and, to her, it was a harsh and ugly sound. She never played the record again. Nothing could be done about it but she never reconciled herself to old age. It brought none of its charms to Oda.

Eventually she accepted her different voice and took pride in the fact that she was still performing. She would listen to a broadcast and confide, "That song is really too much for me, I had to fake it a little." Once, during a broadcast, she moved to the piano and tapped an F: "These notes should be sung loudly but I just touch them, no one notices." She added, "When I am dead they will realize no one has sung for as long as I." That was also an inference to the fact that no one knew her real age.

Mr Barrington-Coupe did not share her reservations about the record and quickly arranged for her to start recording another, also to be prefaced by a recital at the Wigmore Hall. The BBC decided she was not finished after all and invited her to broadcast on the Third Programme. Right until her final hospitalization she was a regular contributor.

She drifted into an Indian Summer of a career and enjoyed every moment. She also undertook a demanding recording schedule, full details of which are given later. Not for Slobodskaya respectable retirement once her voice was past its best, she sang her heart out. No request for a recital, broadcast or lecture was refused, no matter how far she had to travel. It seemed she was compensating for the years in oblivion. As long as she had the strength to stand (and sometimes when she could not, she gave a few recitals sitting in a chair due to ill health) she sang.

CHAPTER TWELVE

HER DEATH WAS announced over the radio and *The Times,*
Daily Telegraph, The Guardian and *The Stage* carried obituary
notices as, in due course, did the music magazines.

The end had been dreadful. For some years she had suffered
from diabetes and an ulcerated foot, which became consistently
more painful. Eventually gangrene set in and she was admitted
to hospital where the foot was amputated. This did not arrest the
infection, so further amputations followed; the leg was removed
below the knee and then the whole limb taken away.

It was then discovered that her other leg was infected and that
this must also be removed. At first she refused and it was
explained if she did not have the amputation her whole system
would be poisoned and she would die. She was distraught. "I do
not want to live my life in a wheelchair," she said. "But I do not
want to die either. Life is sweet."

She gave her consent and the second leg was amputated. Shortly
after, on 29 July 1970, she died at the Royal London Homeopathic
Hospital.

PART THREE

Analysis :
The Artist
Recordings
Discography

THE ARTIST

ODA SLOBODSKAYA HAD a technique that was so secure it enabled her to give concerts when in her 70s. Even in her 80s, when in hospital with her fatal illness, she was making recital plans for her recovery.

Ivor Newton considered her career longevity due to her "great intelligence". He meant that she used her voice wisely and did not overstrain, and this had always been Oda's policy. Even at the conservatoire she refused to eat things which might scratch her throat, and it was a standing joke that any liquid she drank must not exceed 60° in temperature, so as to obviate any risk of scalding.

Accepting she took exceptional care of her instrument, the fact that she sang for so long is testimony to her general hardiness. As Desmond Shawe-Taylor says, "She was as strong as a horse."

In her prime Slobodskaya was cosmopolitan in her choice of music but ultimately she chose to specialize in Russian song (with the exception of Chopin's songs which are Polish). Some of these are not too demanding technically so she was able to relax and give full rein to her imagination. She is now chiefly remembered for introducing these lovely songs to British audiences.

From a purely vocal viewpoint some of these songs should not, some might say, have been attempted publicly. In some of the more taxing passages her delivery, due to advanced age, was not always reliable. Sometimes flaws were exposed. No one was more aware of this than Slobodskaya although she would never admit it to anyone but the closest friends. She would carry on regardless and had such a compelling presence that if audiences noticed, they did not seem to mind.

A peculiarity of her voice was the break between registers which is even slightly apparent in some of her earlier recordings. It seems likely that Slobodskaya's registers were trained singly, which encourages this. In the early years of the century a register

break, or "gear change", was highly fashionable. As the gramophone demonstrates, nearly all the great divas since the history
of recorded sound had register breaks. Patti, Boninsegna, Calvé,
and Butt all changed registers and sometimes in what seems to us
today an alarmingly abrupt manner.

Slobodskaya, naturally, had seen Melba perform (and had
remarked "to tell you the truth I did not think she was very
good") and when she started her own European career it is
natural she should sing in the manner of the established stars of
the period.

In old age the lower section of Slobodskaya's voice became
divorced from the rest and became almost a separate entity. It is
interesting to compare her two recordings of Ippolitoff-Ivanov's
"Reminiscences". The 1939 version shows the registers distinct
but not emphatically so. In the 1959 version the lower register has
become separate. Age did not affect this marvellous lower
register at all, if anything it was even stronger in her later years.
This was not always a good thing as it made the voice appear
"pear" shaped and the top even thinner and more white.

Ivor Newton points out that most established singers stick to a
limited and well-proven repertoire and do not introduce new
music. Slobodskaya did not come into this category. Throughout
her career she sang new material and was always searching for
songs. The Shostakovitch songs, which she added to her
repertoire in 1961, were given her by the composer. Christopher
Raeburn, her Decca producer, recalls that when she came to
record these she found one or two of the lines a little taxing so a
pencilled alteration appeared on the manuscript, shortening some
of the notes. She insisted Shostakovitch himself had done this:
"Look," she said, "he has initialled it." She pointed to the letters
DC. (Shostakovitch is spelled with a C in its Russian fo rm.)
Mr Raeburn pointed out this was not the composer's initialsbut
the musical instruction Da Capo (return to the beginning).
Actually, she was probably joking as she knew full well that Mr
Raeburn was only too aware of the significance of Da Capo, and
no one was more slavishly dedicated to following composers'
instructions than she.

Oda did not stick to the safe, and well-tried, field of bel canto,
but constantly studied new musical forms. She intrepidly entered
the realms of "Sprechgesang" and the chromatic scale, and in the

latter, atonal music, her register breaks were a decided asset. As a student remarked after one of her lecture-recitals, "she goes up and down awfully well".

One of her greatest regrets was that she did not introduce Prokofiev's *Chatterbox* to Britain. She studied this for months, determined not to perform it until she was note perfect. Before this happened Galina Vishnevskaya recorded it.

In the concert hall she could evoke a nostalgic or humorous atmosphere at will. Those who do not think a recital can have its light-hearted moments have obviously never seen Slobodskaya perform.

She was in great demand as a lecturer to conservatoires, colleges and universities; she went down well with the young who probably liked her unorthodox manner.

For one of these lectures she contacted Ivor Newton. "Help me," she said. "I must give a recital and I need a friend." It was clear from her voice over the telephone that she was ill. Mr Newton agreed to accompany her and, when the time came, helped her into the car. "I could not help noticing how frail she looked," he said. "I wondered why she bothered to do it, it wasn't as though she was getting a thousand pounds, or even a hundred for that matter." Her health did not improve during the journey and Mr Newton had grave fears as to the wisdom of her even stepping on to the platform.

But she was insistent and would not give in. She belligerently called for a chair and a table to be put on to the platform and this was done. As always an audience acted like an injection with her. She slowly came to life, sang over a dozen songs, and left the stage smiling and full of energy.

This was part of her art, her special ability; she needed to be the centre of attention and rose magnificently to the occasion. By the same yardstick, dire things could happen if she was not the focal point. Again Ivor Newton supplies the information and recalls Oda attending a party of his. A West End actress was also there and she was holding forth on her play which was enjoying a success. Oda sat sullenly in her chair for about half an hour then claimed she felt ill and left.

Slobodskaya's voice was particularly beautiful and, untypically of Russian females, free of wobble or vibrato because of Iretskaya's method. As stated, the top was the first to show signs of wear. The reason for this is that her highest notes were created artificially by Iretskaya. The artificial portion was exquisite but delicate as china, and although she used it with restraint ultimately it disappeared (notably after the high and sustained tessitura of Salome) leaving her natural voice which was mezzo in range if not in colour. This lack of high notes was a contributory reason why she did so little opera. In her songs she could, and did, omit those troublesome high Bs and Cs. One evening she confessed that if she had her career over again she would concentrate on a mezzo's repertoire. As it was she sang a great deal of mezzo material.

Although Slobodskaya recorded the Letter Scene from Tchaikovsky's *Eugene Onegin*, it is ironic that she is always associated with the rôle of Tatiana. It has even been said she was the world's greatest Tatiana. In fact, she never sang the rôle outside Russia. Yet, she would frequently reminisce how she had performed the part at the Marynsky, sitting at Tatiana's desk with the pen poised in her hand while singing and then writing furiously during the orchestral passages. Today, with the accent on realism, singers try to combine the writing with the singing which may be an advantage if done successfully. To Slobodskaya's way of thinking the all-important thing was the sound, the acting was secondary. She would not dream of jogging her abdomen by writing when in the middle of an aria.

Towards the very end of her career she limited her recital songs to *Katushka*, and a couple of folk songs by Blanter plus one or two miscellaneous items when in the mood to sing them. Her accompanist, however, had to travel with a mountain of music because she could never make up her mind what she would sing until she was on stage. Sometimes she would ask for requests and select those she thought she could manage. Friends were invariably scattered in the audience and shouted out those with which they knew she would be happy. Not that anyone would have dared to confess that to her.

She steadfastly refused to transpose. This could be nerve-racking for anyone in her company a few days prior to a performance as she would suddenly, when it was least expected, try out a few of the higher notes. She would push the tone so far forward into the mask that it became a shrill whistle. The effect on someone performing some unrelated task, when this ear-splitting whistle was delivered fortissimo and apropos of nothing, could be shattering.

She had her champions and nearly all the respected critics were among these. Andrew Porter gave her a great deal of encouragement when she made her come-back and when asked to contribute to this book wrote:

"She had a wonderful sense of line—joining one note to the next without holes, giving each the right weight and timing. When she saw me she used to say 'Ah, Andrew Porter, who admires my gloooooorrrrious legaaaaato'. I loved the personality she brought to her singing; the sound of her voice. I'm glad someone is writing about her."

RECORDINGS

SLOBODSKAYA'S FIRST RECORDING sessions were for HMV and took place in the February of 1931 at the small Queen's Hall. Accompanied by Percy Kahn she made matrixes of Gretchaninoff's "Lullaby"; two Tchaikovsky songs, "So Soon Forgotten" and "Was I Not Like a Tender Blade of Grass?"; Rachmaninov's "Lilacs"; Rubinstein's "Roses"; and Parassia's aria from Mussorgsky's *Sorochinsky Fair*.

She was 42 at the time and sounds much younger, she is confident, secure and unhampered by laboured production. There is no evidence of breaks between the registers.

The Gretchaninoff and Tchaikovsky songs have never been issued commercially which is tragic as they are, quite simply, superb. The latter three items were issued in 1931 on the HMV Plum Label 10" 78rpm EK 113.

"Roses" was written for Iretskaya and is never heard nowadays, but "Lilacs" crops up from time to time and has recently been recorded by Elisabeth Soderstrom (SXL 6832), and there is the exciting Nina Koshetz version which was reissued in 1978. "Lilacs" is full of the tender impetuosity of first love and contains some interesting Russian nasal vowels, which, in fact, are attractive. The high notes are elegantly bowed. "Roses" owes much of its flavour to the orient, particularly in the minor cadences which can be heard in some of Rimsky-Korsakov's songs. Slobodskaya's line is faultless throughout and the rich, lower portion of her voice is well illustrated as she performs some stylish octave descents.

Sorochinsky Fair has a lyrical opening, showing a facet of Mussorgsky which is not over-abundant, and Slobodskaya sustains some perfect pianissimos on high As and Bs. The second half of the aria sounds a little bizarre with its staccato semiquavers sung in synchronization with the piano, and it is an object lesson in timing. As Slobodskaya used to say, "That's not as easy as it sounds."

EK 113 is Slobodskaya's finest record but, sadly, it did not sell well. When she tried to persuade HMV executives to record her again she was told there was no market for her repertoire but, if she was prepared to pay the expenses, HMV would make the recordings for her. She declined.

Scarcely less lovely is the Rimington van Wyck set comprising four 12" 78rpm records made in 1938, in which she is accompanied by Ivor Newton. Her own favourite recording, Tchaikovsky's "Golden Cornfields", is included in this collection. Sir Compton Mackenzie reviewed the set for *The Gramophone*:

It is not only a glorious voice. Many have had that and fallen by the wayside. It is used, this voice, with a perfection of technique that stands out like a beacon of light in the well-nigh total darkness. To this grand artist florid passages come as easily as the finely spun legato or the generous flow of tone she uses. She can use a delicious parlando or a delicate touch on a curving phrase of melody, and she can rise superbly to a big, dramatic climax or confidently tackle a sudden precipitous note. This is, in fact, the perfect technical control.

The Rimington van Wyck set was recorded due to the efforts of Mr Fred Smith who was connected with the famous Rimington van Wyck record shop in Leicester Square, now renamed and owned by EMI. Mr Smith was an idealist with a great love for fine singing. He fell in love with Slobodskaya's voice after hearing one of her radio recitals, and telephoned her the same day asking if she would like to record for him, the choice of material to be left to her.

Instead of jumping at the opportunity, she demurred. She had heard that Decca, under whose banner the Rimington van Wyck set would appear, was not as prestigious as HMV, therefore she was not sure if it would be wise to associate herself with the company. That HMV had shown no interest in her for seven years in no way influenced her argument. Everyone she knew had to be questioned at length as to whether or not she should allow Decca to record her. Fortunately her friends urged her to accept.

So the recordings were made and issued in a limited edition of 2,000 copies, bearing a classy orange label:

That recording session proved an inspiration [she wrote]. I was in good form and my voice was at its best. Fred Smith would come out of the studios after a session, pale and emotional, murmuring "It was so beautiful, so beautiful". The memory of that pale face, sometimes with a tear in the eye, will never be forgotten.

The above was written in retrospect. At the time of their issue Slobodskaya publicly proclaimed she did not like the records. And when she was the subject of *Desert Island Discs* on 5 December 1960 she told Roy Plomley, "The only thing I liked about the records was Fred Smith's enthusiasm." Nevertheless she chose "Golden Cornfields" as one of the eight discs she would take to the island with her, and if only one was allowed, that would have been it.

The Rimington van Wyck set captures Slobodskaya in her vocal prime, she was just 50, and at her interpretative best. Ivor Newton, her accompanist, is sensitive and supportive. Sadly, the material of which the records were made, shellac, did not match up to her artistry. It was of poor quality, full of surface noise and not durable. Even if a RvW set can be discovered nowadays, and it is exceedingly rare, the records may be seriously impaired.

So successful was the Rimington van Wyck set that Decca arranged another recording session with her, this time the records to be issued in a straight-forward way under the usual Decca label.

She chose songs by Ippolitoff-Ivanov, Gretchaninoff, Rimsky-Korsakov, Borodin and Balakirev and recorded sufficient material to fill two 12″ 78s, but only one record was issued. Eventually the matrix for the other record became lost in the confusion of war.

In 1945 she was again invited to record for Decca, this time a full-scale operatic aria, the Letter Scene from Tchaikovsky's *Eugene Onegin*. She was to be accompanied by the London Symphony Orchestra under Anatole Fistoulari.

Slobodskaya was 57 and her voice had taken a mezzo quality and is altogether darker than on the RvW set. But, as might be expected, the aria is impeccably sung, particularly the introspective middle section, and there is no version to rival it. Technically, there is the slightest trace of "blast" on her high B flat, but it does not deter from the performance.

It was planned, originally, to issue the Letter Scene as a set of two 12" 78rpm records, yet it was not issued in this form, and, as with previous recordings, became lost. Slobodskaya blamed Decca for not issuing the record straight away, but there is another side to the story. Being a perfectionist she was unhappy about the B flat and refused to sign a release form, hanging on to the belief that she could force Decca into another session to remedy the fault. By the time she realized Decca would not relent and that she had made a mistake, it was too late and the matrix had become lost in the upheaval of rehousing the archives during the war.

Two composers wrote songs specially for Slobodskaya, these were Gretchaninoff and Medtner. Both were self-imposed exiles from Russia. Gretchaninoff gave her "The Dreary Steppes", one of her greatest record successes, and Medtner wrote songs for her which she recorded in 1947.

Although Gretchaninoff had taught at the St Petersburg Conservatoire for a while, under Rimsky-Korsakov, he had left by the time Slobodskaya started her studies, so she did not meet him until her days in America, and it was there that he gave her the manuscript for "The Dreary Steppes". She met him for the last time in 1954, in Paris, on his 90th birthday.

Gretchaninoff's songs are not much sung, which is a pity as they are full of melody, emotion and charm. It is possibly this that has damned them in contemporary musical circles. Medtner's music is quite different. He is complex, difficult to understand and hard on the ear, like maths put to music. The story of how his work came to be recorded reads like a fairy tale.

He enjoyed a considerable success in Russia before the revolution, but decided to leave after the new régime seized power. He left his homeland in 1920 and wandered about the world before settling in England in 1936. He came to England because, as Oda said endearingly "it is an hospitable country". He received little acclaim but, despite this, continued to compose prolifically. In addition to composition, he was a highly talented virtuoso pianist, but his style was considered too original and his engagements were few.

In its desire to cater for minority tastes, the BBC arranged for a recital of his music to be broadcast on the World Service. The Medtner recital was picked up in India by the Maharajah of

Mysore. The Maharajah was intrigued by the strange, extravagant music and contacted HMV, in Britain, with instructions to ship all Medtner recordings to him, in India. Great was his surprise when the answer came that no Medtner recordings had been made. Being a maharajah, and possessing a fortune, he dealt with the matter in a speedy and practical way. If there were no recordings available, then some must be made. He ordered Medtner's entire repertoire to be recorded at his expense. HMV were only too delighted to comply. There were a considerable number of songs among Medtner's output and that is where Slobodskaya came in:

> I have always held his music in the highest esteem [she said]. Although, when I was young I considered it way above my head and was afraid to sing it. His songs are difficult to perform and can only ever be sung by singers of musical maturity.
> Although I listened with reverence, nearer to my heart was the music of Tchaikovsky, he brought tears to my eyes because his appeal is immediate.

Even if it was not Tchaikovsky, HMV were offering a contract and that could not be spurned, and she had never hesitated to learn, and sing, difficult music. She had almost met Medtner previously, when the cellist Belousoff had been about to introduce them:

> He got me as far as the door when I turned tail and fled, terrified at the thought of meeting Medtner without knowing his music sufficiently well.
> I had heard his songs, and they were complicated, and I certainly did not know them well enough to sing in front of him, as he would probably ask. So I escaped. Was I stupid, or just shy?

Later, however, Slobodskaya and Medtner did meet:

> When I knew I possessed more musical baggage I studied Medtner's music and prepared a programme of his songs. Then I approached him and asked if I might sing them for him and that, if he approved, perhaps he might accompany me at a concert.

He seemed pleased with me and agreed, so, of course, endless rehearsals followed, most of which were held at his home. Anna Mikhailovna, Medtner's wife, was always with us, preparing pampoushetski for us to eat—God forbid we should be hungry.

Anna Mikhailovna seems to have been a good natured sort, devoted to her husband and well able to contend with the odd flare-up between the composer and opera singer. A case in question concerned their respective dignities. Slobodskaya's version goes:

Medtner refused to turn the pages of his music in case he should miss one precious note of his accompaniment (and there are so many notes in his accompaniment) and I would not turn the pages in case I interrupted the thread of the song. Anna Mikhailovna knew every note of her husband's music and, at the right moment, would rush in from the kitchen, frying pan in hand, in order to be in time to turn the page.

The Medtner songs Slobodskaya recorded for HMV are "To A Dreamer", "The Ravens", "Serenade", "I Cannot Bear to Hear the Birds", "Life's Waggon", "Spring Solace" and "Willow, Why Forever Bending?" They are the rarest of all Slobodskaya recordings and, it appears, nobody sings the songs at all nowadays. Medtner himself seems to have slipped into the limbo of lost composers.

As Medtner was primarily a composer for the piano, the piano part dominates the song, and the singer plays a secondary rôle. The vocal line is stretched over an elaborate framework of accompaniment. This, on first hearing, makes the songs appear unbalanced. Whereas not atonal, neither are they lyrical; they are as near abstract as a song can get. A trademark of Medtner's songs are the unexpected, precipitate intervals which call for enormous agility from the singer.

"Willow, Why Forever Bending?" is typical of the output of its idiosyncratic composer. Slobodskaya interprets it with creamy, smooth legato and extracts every nuance of lyricism from the fragmentary phrases. Her breath control is iron-clad and her 40 years of experience show through.

"Life's Waggon" has complicated, florid passages which have
to be sung loudly and during which it would be all too easy to
skid out of control. There is a central motif which is plaintively
reflected at the end, and Oda holds her soft line unwaveringly
until the piano rumbles to a stop. Her tone is full but never too
heavy for the baroque phrasing.

"Spring Solace" is a gift for her with its opening notes below
the stave, allowing her to show off her chest register. This could
cause grave difficulties for many sopranos, and be unsingable for
a singer such as Joan Hammond, who had an excellent and
liquid top, but not too much beneath.

Slobodskaya did not record again after the Medtner set until
1959, a gap of twelve years, and then Mr Barrington-Coupe
approached her on behalf of Saga Records. And what can be said
of these records? Her voice certainly appears worn, strained and
perilously thin on top. Her artistry, though, shines through the
blemishes and what is left of the voice is full-blooded and, as long
as she does not sing above the stave, beautiful. She has trouble
with her breath in one or two items, such as the well-known "The
Lark Sings Louder", from Rimsky-Korsakov's cycle "In Spring",
where the line disintegrates into an inaudible mumble. But there
is no rule that folk songs may only be approached by the young;
the idea is to convey the message of the song, and this she does
brilliantly whether it be love, loneliness or bereavement. Her
version of "None But The Lonely Heart" is superb and almost
masculine in its strength, with no trace of mawkishness.

Two formidable Mussorgsky cycles dominate the Saga records
and these are *The Nursery* and *The Sunless*.

The Nursery is a series of psychological sketches showing the
relationship between a child and his old nanny; it also shows how
far ahead of his time was the composer. The songs vary from cute
to semi-tragic and Slobodskaya sails through them with great
panache. She is equally impressive with the sombre *The Sunless*,
creating the correct, forbidding atmosphere from the start.

The Saga records re-launched Slobodskaya as a recording and
concert artist and as a result she increased her number of public
appearances. Consequently her technique snapped back into
action and her voice regained some of its quality.

Even a cursory hearing of side two of the Decca *The Art of
Oda Slobodskaya*, recorded in 1961, reveals that she is in much

finer form than on the Saga records made two years earlier. *The Art of Oda Slobodskaya* came about after her Saga records had been well received and Decca considered she might now be a marketable proposition.

The producers set about assembling the record in a rather charming way. Quite unexpectedly, Oda received an invitation to lunch with certain Decca officials at their offices on the Thames Embankment. She had no idea what was required of her but suspected it would be something to her advantage. After a "splendid lunch" her hosts invited her to step into an adjacent studio and give her valued opinion on a new singer whom they were considering recording. She was flattered by this and settled herself comfortably while a tape was played. The familiar opening bars of the Letter Scene came from the speakers. She nearly fell off the chair with shock when the singer came in, as it was her own voice. So many emotions surged through her she simply burst into tears. She knew that that particular recording, made in 1945, with the London Symphony Orchestra under Fistoulari, had been lost when Decca moved its archives during the war.

Gently it was explained to her that a mammoth sorting out of matrixes had taken place in the archives and the Letter Scene, together with other recordings she had made, had been discovered among a heap of discarded matrixes which were unlabelled and relegated for destruction. But someone had played a matrix out of curiosity, and recognized her voice. After a laborious process of cleaning and polishing it was confirmed that the matrixes were undamaged, and it was then a simple matter to dub them on to tape.

Decca planned to issue the Letter Scene on a LP, together with the other recordings they had unearthed, which included the settings of folk songs by Ippolitoff-Ivanov. As there were only enough items for one side, it was hoped that the reverse would be original material which she would shortly record in the Decca studios. Was she interested?

For the "new" side of the LP she chose songs by Tchaikovsky, Rachmaninov, Prokofiev, Blanter and Stravinsky, some of which had already been recorded by Saga.

Christopher Raeburn was producing her sessions and she fell in love with him, which is probably a contributory reason why she worked so well. He was so considerate she could not resist him.

She dare not declare her passion as he was a married man, and Oda could be quite proper about that sort of thing, so she poured out her heart to her diary. In an effort to attract his interest she bought herself a new pink cardigan and some red boots. Mr Raeburn still remembers those boots and remarked that they were so characteristic he thought of retitling the record "Marching With Oda".

It was Christopher Raeburn who suggested Slobodskaya's spoken introductions to some of her songs, and these are enormously successful.

Desmond Shawe-Taylor reviewed *The Art* for *The Gramophone* and, after enthusing over side one, remarks:

> . . . the great joy of the record is the second side which catches the singer in far better form than she showed on either of the Saga records. In fact, she sounds quite brilliant . . . [her voice is] dark and full blooded with that impeccable legato which should be the envy and admiration of every young soprano in the country.

She was delighted with that and forever after it was "that nice Mr Shawe-Taylor".

At the same session she recorded some song cycles by Shostakovitch and Kabalevsky, but these were unissued until 1962 when they appeared as two separate 7″ Extended Play records. Desmond Shawe-Taylor also reviewed these:

> As for two 7″ records by Oda Slobodskaya, words fail me—as they never fail her. One of the Kabalevsky nursery songs is prefixed by her own account of its content, which is so priceless in its vitality and fun that I simply can't resist playing it to anyone who comes into the house. Her actual singing, both in this cycle and in the companion set of Shostakovitch's Six Spanish Songs is of startling brilliance and beauty while as an interpreter she is simply unique. There are times when I am tempted to call her the greatest singer now living.

Around 1964, it is difficult to be more specific, she recorded the narration for Prokofiev's *Peter and the Wolf*, and there is no doubt

that this would not have come about but for Christopher Raeburn's brainwave in encouraging her spoken introductions. The
orchestration for this recording is termed the Colonne Orchestra
conducted by Issaie Disenhaus. Unfortunately the playing is dull
and uninspired, and the recording flat and muted. All of which
is in contrast to Slobodskaya's colourful story-telling. When the
Sunday Times critic wrote of her performance of *Peter and the Wolf*
at the Royal Festival Hall in the May of 1964 "Colourful narrator
Oda Slobodskaya immediately filled the hall with her presence"
it is quite clear, after listening to the record, exactly what he
meant.

That same year she recorded the complete songs of Chopin,
nineteen in all, which she sang in the original Polish, taking the
trouble to have Polish lessons before she made the record. Yet
again Desmond Shawe-Taylor is enthusiastic: "Oda Slobodskaya
has recorded the entire set of Chopin songs in a masterly style . . .
such is her vitality and attack and rhythmic zest that no thought
of tedium can arise."

Despite this gallantry, and accepting that the songs are enthusiastically sung, and that her tone is perfectly steady, there is
no doubt it is an old, and rather battered, voice singing them.

After her death, Revolution Records re-issued the Chopin
songs in an album entitled *Memorial Album Oda Slobodskaya*. It
is a pathetic memorial to the great singer to re-issue examples of
her art recorded when she was 76 years old, but it was the only
matrix available to the company at that time. But what is exciting
is the companion E.P. ($33\frac{1}{3}$) issued with the *Memorial*. This
contains five songs by Glinka and Dargomijsky.

Recorded after the Chopin songs, when she was nearly 80,
these are her last-known recordings, and her voice is superb. She
seems to have discarded old age and is full of energy and style.
Of course, the lovely gold-spun thread of her earlier tone has
been replaced by a darker, steelier and more restricted sound but
this is still beautiful, and used expertly; there are no idiosyncrasies
or tricks, it is just straight-forward, good singing.

The Glinka and Dargomijsky songs are miniature masterpieces,
fresh and instantly appealing. It seems odd that British audiences
never get a chance to hear these songs in the recital hall when we
have a surfeit of lieder that is constantly performed. The difficulty
of the Russian language cannot be the barrier as most British

concert-goers do not understand German but this does not detract from the popularity of lieder. Now that Slobodskaya is dead, it will probably be a long time, if ever, before anyone performs these songs again.

The tape containing these songs was discovered by accident, and arrived at the offices of Revolution Records together with the master tapes for the Chopin songs. Apparently they had been stored together. Slobodskaya's voice was immediately recognized as was the crisp piano accompaniment of Frederick Stone, but the songs were so rare it took considerable research to have them identified.

There are three songs by Glinka, "Doubt", "Gretchen's Song" from *Faust*, and "Illinishna's Song" from *Prince Kholansky*.

In "Doubt" her line is superb and the voice supple. Each phrase is treated individually, even when the notation is the same, and the listener feels, instinctively, that this is the way Glinka meant it to be. There is no need for a translation as, right from the beginning, Slobodskaya pours meaning into every yearning word. Her opening attack is so refined that it seems the voice, and the piano, are one instrument.

The *Faust* item is full of self-questioning, and spans a wide vocal palette, but the voice is integrated and there is no undue unbalance, or heaviness, in the lower register. If her voice had continued to improve at this rate, by the time she was 100 she would have been singing Tatiana again. After the moderately paced opening, the melody accelerates into waltz time, and the voice opens with great power which is sustained throughout the song.

"Illinishna's Song" is a peasant folk tune and Slobodskaya wrings every ounce from the bouncy melody; she is entirely at home. This is the old lady trundling home from market with a sack of potatoes on her back and not giving a damn for anyone. A character not entirely unknown to Slobodskaya.

The Dargomijsky songs are lyrical, and he was a composer with whom she always felt an affinity. "Little Cloud in the Sky" is far from easy to sing, due to its florid line, almost coloratura, which was not Slobodskaya's métier at all. But she proves she can be equal to the task if she has to be, and each demi-semi-quaver is touched crisply, there is no skidding down the long phrases and her breath control is remarkable. On some of the higher phrases the voice bursts open at the top of the line, like a shower of bright sparks, but she does not lose control for an instant. The precarious intervals contained in this song might well cause a newcomer to pause, but she is far too old a stager to run into difficulties there.

"When I Was Sixteen" is this reviewer's favourite Slobodskaya recording. It is overly romantic and could, so easily, degenerate into coquetry in less capable hands. The spoken introduction, wisdom commenting on youth, is the whole essence of Richard Strauss' Marschallin summed up in a single song. There is no other singer who could treat the song as does Slobodskaya, and get away with it. It is expressive, gentle and full of concern with waves of pathos washing over it. It is the encapsulation of her art.

DISCOGRAPHY

THIS LIST SOLELY refers to commercial recordings. In addition, there are various private tapes of Slobodskaya, and the British Institute of Recorded Sound houses several recorded lecture-recitals made between 1947 and 1966. The BBC Sound Archives also hold master tapes of broadcast recitals. All items are sung in Russian unless otherwise stated.

Issued 1931
HMV EK 113: 10" 78rpm
Rachmaninov: Lilacs. *Rubinstein:* Roses. *Mussorgsky:* Parassia's aria from *Sorochinsky Fair.*

Issued 1938
DECCA RVW 104/7: Four 12" 78rpm
RVW 104
Tanejev: Nocturne. *Tchaikovsky:* Was I Not Like A Tender Blade Of Grass.
RVW 105
Tanejev: Dreams. My Heart Is Throbbing. In The Silence Of The Night. *Tcherepnin:* I Would Have Kissed You.
RVW 106
Rachmaninov: Lilacs. How Lovely Here. *Cui:* The Statue. *Tchaikovsky:* So Soon Forgotten.
RVW 107
Tchaikovsky: The Golden Cornfields. If Only I Had Known.

Issued 1939
DECCA K 1206 12" 78rpm
Gretchaninoff: The Dreary Steppes. *Borodin:* From My Tears Spring Flowers. *Balakirev:* Hebrew Melody.

Issued 1947
Gramophone DB 6565 12" 78rpm

Medtner: To A Dreamer (Reverse not Slobodskaya).
Gramophone DB 6906 12" 78rpm
Medtner: The Ravens. Serenade. I Cannot Bear To Hear The
Birds.

Issued 1959 LP *Russian Songs* Vol. 1.
SAGA XID 5050
Mussorgsky: The Nursery Suite. *Glinka:* Star Of The North.
Travelling Song. *Dargomijsky:* I Love Him Still. The Capricious
Wife. *Tchaikovsky:* Not A Word. Ballroom Meeting. Lullaby In
A Storm.

Issued 1959 LP *Russian Songs* Vol. II.
SAGA XID 5069
Mussorgsky: Sunless Cycle. The Magpie. The Orphan. Where Art
Thou Little Star. Hopak. Gathering Mushrooms. *Borodin:* Rich
And Poor. False Note. From My Tears Sprang Flowers. The
Sleeping Princess. *Rimsky-Korsakov:* The Hills of Georgia. The
Lark Sings Louder. *Ippolitoff-Ivanov:* Reminiscences. I'm Sitting
On A Stone. The Merry Wife. *Rimsky-Korsakov:* Cradle Song.
The Nightingale And The Rose. *Blanter:* In the Front Line.
Katushka. The Little Light.

Issued 1961
DECCA LXT 5663 LP *The Art of Oda Slobodskaya*
DECCA SXL 2299 (stereo)
Ippolitoff-Ivanov: Reminiscences. I'm Sitting On A Stone. The
Merry Wife. *Gretchaninoff:* Lullaby. The Dreary Steppes. Like An
Angel. My Country. *Borodin:* From My Tears Spring Flowers.
Water Nymphs. *Balakirev:* Hebrew Melody (All Recorded 1939).
Tchaikovsky: The Letter Scene from "Eugene Onegin" (Recorded
1945). Child Song. *Rachmaninov:* To The Children. The Island.
The Soldier's Wife. *Prokofiev:* Dunyushka. *Blanter:* In The Front
Line. Katushka. *Stravinsky:* Three Children's Songs. (All
Recorded 1961).

Issued 1962
DECCA CEP 5500 7" EP 45rpm
Shostakovitch: Six Spanish Songs.

DECCA CEP 5501 7" EP 45rpm
Kabalevsky: Seven Nursery Rhymes.

Issued 1964
FIDELIO ATL 4102 LP *Peter and the Wolf.*
Prokofiev: Peter And The Wolf. Narration in English (Other side
not Slobodskaya).
DELTA DEL 12004 LP "Chopin Songs".
Chopin: Nineteen Polish Songs. (Sung in Polish)

Issued 1971
REVOLUTION RCF 011 LP *Memorial Album Oda Slobodskaya.*
Chopin: Nineteen Polish Songs.
Coupled with companion 33⅓ EP.
Glinka: Doubt. Gretchen's Song. Illinishna's Song. *Dargomijsky:*
Little Cloud. When I Was Sixteen.

Issued 1973
SAGA 5357 LP *Oda Slobodskaya Sings Mussorgsky.*
Mussorgsky: Sunless Cycle. The Nursery Suite. Where Art Thou
Little Star. Hopak. Gathering Mushrooms. The Orphan. The
Magpie.

PART FOUR

Memories

DAME EVA TURNER

I WELCOME AND am utterly delighted to have this chance of recalling my association with Oda Slobodskaya, the supreme interpreter of Russian repertoire. She was a remarkable person, tall of bearing in every sense of the word, full of intensity, and dramatic, even in her everyday conversation.

We are indebted and grateful to her for the privilege and pleasure of having heard much Russian music that otherwise might have been denied us. But I also recall how she covered herself with glory in non-Russian rôles, notably during the 1935 Covent Garden season under Sir Thomas Beecham, when she interpreted the rôle of Palmyra in Delius's *Koanga*. We became friends, as I also took part in that season, having just returned from Milano to sing Amelia in *Un Ballo in Maschera*.

I vividly recollect her numerous promenade concerts and the occasion that she came so generously, and willingly, to sing for the Royal Academy of Music Club when I was Professor of Voice there.

How can one sum up her artistry? She had the ability of making words pregnant with meaning and getting to the heart of the work. Her voice was exquisite and had a certain clarion ring about it which pronounced it at once Russian.

We were all enriched by her presence, and will not forget her.

MR IVOR NEWTON

AGE, OTHER PEOPLE's as well as her own, was a topic never to be discussed in her presence, and she never seemed to grow old. She was well over 70 when, in 1961, we made our final records of Russian songs together, in which her singing received great praise, and since then I remember several concerts and lecture-recitals at which, as full as ever of enormous vitality, she captured, dominated and delighted audiences.

At the City of London Festival in 1964, she was in splendid form and after singing three or four encores she turned to me and said "Let us give them some Mussorgsky now". I suggested that it might be a good thing if she stopped while everyone was clamouring for more, and she at once turned to the audience and said, dejectedly, "Ivor says I'm not to sing any more." Of course, my advice was over-ridden by everybody present!

Slobodskaya had an infinite capacity for study. No one ever found greater pleasure in learning, rehearsing and adding to her repertory. It was not only that she loved to find unfamiliar, old works in familiar idioms, but that all her life she maintained an insatiable appetite for new music, and always kept in touch with new works from Russia. Her scholarship in this respect did not inhibit her appeal to an audience.

During the last, terrible, year of her life, when lying in hospital, she was subject to bouts of agonizing pain, I could not but tell her how I admired her courage. "When pain comes," she replied, "I go through my repertory—one day Mussorgsky, another Rachmaninov, another Tchaikovsky, another Prokofiev. I grow so angry with myself if I have forgotten a word . . . I could not stand the pain if it were not for that."

I have memories, not just of her lovely singing, but her colourful personality. Life is certainly duller without her. I have never known such a forceful personality, or such a zest for life.

Reprinted by kind permission of
Opera magazine.

MISS RICCA FOX

Russian-born Ricca Fox had a distinguished career as a concert pianist until an accident to her right arm curtailed this. Since then she has specialized as a rehearsal pianist, and was connected with many Diaghilev productions. She has worked closely with Slobodskaya on many occasions.

I FIRST MET her in Berlin in 1922. By that time many refugees had started to trickle in from Russia. She was not beautiful to look at but was slender, with a good figure, and that made her appear tall. When I think back I can visualize her.

We appeared together at a charity concert and the famous tenor Leonid Sobinov was also there. When she sang her artistry was superb and she knocked the rest of us, Sobinov included, into a cocked hat. Elisabeth Schwarzkopf is a great interpretative artist but, for my money, Slobodskaya was better. She had greatness and could have conquered the world but she had principles, as I later discovered in America.

She never sang with the Metropolitan Opera in New York but she had the opportunity. One of the directors took a great fancy to her and offered her the Metropolitan if she would live with him. But he already had a wife and children and she would not break up the marriage. How many others do you know who would have behaved like that? Most singers would do anything to get to the Metropolitan.

Later, in England, we were both connected with *Sorochinsky Fair*. By this time she had become a little unsure of herself as her voice was beginning to go—but of all the singers I've known she carried on the longest.

She was always pleasant to me because I was not competition. What she did to competition I do not know, for she had her likes and dislikes, but I don't think she was a bad colleague.

When she started to teach she asked me to play for her students. And I did it for the princely sum of 3/6d [17½p] an hour. Most of the lesson seemed to consist of her singing to the students and then she would invite them to do a little bit. She rarely stopped them if they made mistakes. She was not the best of teachers, no pedagogue.

She could be one of life's grabbers. Not with money, but with your life's blood—she sapped your energy if you had something to give. But whatever her faults, and she was human like the rest of us, when she sang she gave of her best. When she opened her mouth one forgot her plain face, one even forgot the surroundings. I think it could be honestly said she was a genius.

MR DESMOND SHAWE-TAYLOR

HER VOICE WAS characteristically Russian in colour, but without the drawbacks so often found in Russian sopranos. It was equally free from the heavy, unwieldy vibrato we have learned to dread in Slavonic voices, and from pinched or shrill sounds in the upper register. Many Russian singers produced a "squeezed" sound, as though too much volume were being pushed through too small a space, but with Oda one was conscious only of a continuous even pressure that always remained "wide" and easy.

She had a most beautiful legato, a quality that I particularly prize in singers. I remember that once, when we were listening to a record of Mussorgsky songs by a bass, she said, "It's not musical enough, he uses far too much parlando. Instead of a musical line it sounds like a recitative." She preserved that impeccable legato of hers for an enormously long time. In some of her later records she had some difficulty in reaching the higher notes, but she never lost her beautiful line.

All her recordings, whether early or late, are enlivened by her personal qualities: her zest, her energy, her humour and total lack of self-consciousness. In "The Bear" her preliminary account of the old couple, and the terrifying bear looking for the paw that they had cooked, is so rivetting and so wildly funny, that Stravinsky's short setting of the folk song, when it comes, is almost an anticlimax. And who can ever forget her account, both spoken and sung, of the little pig, in the Kabalevsky nursery rhyme, who couldn't say "Chru, chru"?

For a long time she was the outstanding interpreter of Russian song in this country—perhaps the world. Her repertoire was huge and she was never frightened of taking on something entirely new. She has left a gap that has so far proved impossible to fill.

MISS SYLVIA FISHER

SHE HAD a unique approach and would colour her songs, each one differently from the other, according to the mood. Most singers today are just technicians, she was full of colour. There is no mystery as to why she was still singing when in her 70s, if the voice isn't destroyed then there is no reason why one should not sing for ever, and she had the skill not to ill-use her vocal equipment.

I was at her second come-back concert and the thing that most struck me was that she, seemingly, had endless breath. Her line would go on for ever and she would tailor each phrase so elegantly.

So many singers today seem to sound the same with their notes. If a certain note in the scale is produced, say an A, then that A will always be coloured in exactly the same way, if the passage is tender then it will sound piano, if passionate then forte, but the basic sound is unvaried. Not so with Oda who coloured each note individually.

I think that, perhaps, too much emphasis is put on technique today. Of course, there must be a firm foundation for the voice, but after that the artist should use her imagination. The voice can convey so much. Think of Chaliapine, and how he sang, hear him interpret four or five different songs, and you would think it was four or five different singers. The emphasis today is all on the cerebral part of singing. Oda came from a school that encouraged imagination and added to that, she was a true original.

I have many memories of her, but two are outstanding. The first was when she learned I was going to Leningrad with Benjamin Britten, to sing in *Albert Herring*. She got in touch with me and asked me to see one of her sisters, who was still there, and to take her some chocolate. I agreed and a surreptitious meeting was arranged in the hotel lobby, but both her sister and I were terrified. When I went up to my room to get the chocolate I was petrified that an iron hand would suddenly grab me and whisk me off to jail. But it was worth the ordeal as I was able to reassure Oda afterwards, and she had been very concerned.

My other memory is when I went to see her in hospital the day of the amputation of her second leg. The nurse said that I must not speak, but that I could look at her. She looked so forlorn and helpless. I was so upset that I could barely walk from the hospital.

MAESTRO ANATOLE FISTOULARI

She had wonderful diction and was a hard worker who got the full meaning from every syllable she sang. On top of this she had a wonderful voice. I shall never forget some of her lunchtime concerts at the National Gallery, they were perfect.

She wasn't always 100 per cent soft with other artists if things went wrong. She could be a little difficult. Neither did she forget a slight. She once sang for some Russian charity and was presented with a small bouquet, which she accepted with great charm. Years later, I was at the theatre with the lady who had organized the concert and we met Slobodskaya. As they had not actually met before, I introduced them. At once Slobodskaya flared up and rounded on the woman, "How dare you give me that miserable, tuppeny-ha'penny bouquet?" she said. "I have sung at Covent Garden and La Scala, have you no idea how to behave?" The poor woman nearly collapsed and I was left standing with my mouth open. After all, in her way, the woman had tried to be kind. But although it had happened years ago, the incident was still vivid to Oda.

But there were other times when she could be nice and sweet. My daughter, Marina, was just a little girl when we were rehearsing *Eugene Onegin*, and she had no interest in singing at that age. Yet, when Oda sang she rushed into the room shouting "I like it, I like it". Oda was delighted and stopped singing at once, to hug her.

Professionally she had a discipline and she was a good actress who always knew her part perfectly. Everything she sang was full of significance and, although in the last years she lost the top of her voice, her art was always there.

Right after the war I recommended her to some people at Decca, who wanted to record some Russian arias and they asked us to do the Letter Scene.

There was a little difficulty over the high B flat because her range had sunk a little, and I suggested that, perhaps, she transpose that note. "But Tchaikovsky wrote a B flat," she answered, amazed that I should suggest such a thing. "I know what he wrote," I said. "But I was trying to think of you." But she would have none of it. Perhaps that note is a little harsh, even on record, but she would have it no other way. She was a perfectionist.

INDEX

N.B. Composers' names inserted only as they appear in the text.